Women's Cricket and Global Processes

Women's Cricket and Global Processes

The Emergence and Development of Women's Cricket as a Global Game

Philippa Velija
York St John University, UK

First published 2015 by
PALGRAVE MACMILLAN

Palgrave Macmillan in the UK is an imprint of Macmillan Publishers Limited,
registered in England, company number 785998, of Houndmills,
Basingstoke, Hampshire, RG21 6XS.

Palgrave Macmillan in the US is a division of St Martin's Press LLC,
175 Fifth Avenue, New York, NY 10010.

Palgrave Macmillan is the global academic imprint of the above
companies and has companies and representatives throughout the world.

Palgrave® and Macmillan® are registered trademarks in the
United States, the United Kingdom, Europe and other countries.

ISBN: 978–1–137–32351–4

This book is printed on paper suitable for recycling and made from
fully managed and sustained forest sources. Logging, pulping and
manufacturing processes are expected to conform to the environmental
regulations of the country of origin.

A catalogue record for this book is available from the British Library.

Library of Congress Cataloging-in-Publication Data

Velija, Philippa.
   Women's cricket and global processes : the emergence and
development of women's cricket as a global game / Philippa Velija.
      pages   cm
   ISBN 978–1–137–32351–4 (hardback)
   1. Cricket for women.   2. Cricket—Social aspects.   3. Sports and
globalization.   I. Title.
   GV929.V45 2015
   796.358082—dc23   2014049595

For Cimi, Mollie and Merida

Contents

List of Tables

Preface

This book provides a sociological analysis of women's cricket by focusing on understanding the emergence, development and continual issues that enable and constrain the development of women's cricket as a global game. Despite there being extensive academic research on the history and globalisation of men's cricket, little is known about the development and emergence of women's cricket as a global sport. In popular accounts women's cricket is wrongly considered a 'new' sport, one that was developed through men's involvement post-2005. But this is not the case and this book seeks to uncover the social processes involved in the emergence and development of women's cricket and the organisations that govern the game nationally and internationally. Focusing on power relations between men's and women's cricket, this book seeks to explain, firstly, how and why the women's game has developed the way it has, and secondly, how power relations between men's and women's cricket continue to shape the development of the women's game as well as influence the social identities of women who play the 'global game'.

Acknowledgements

Thank you to Cimi, for supporting my academic career; whilst I was writing this book, you were renovating our beautiful home. To my beautiful daughters Mollie and Merida, thank you for the joy and happiness that you bring mummy (and daddy); we are blessed to have you both.

Thank you to my Mum and Dad, John and Colette Cook, who have always supported my academic career: your financial support throughout my studies, help looking after the girls and your encouragement and support have been much appreciated and words are not enough to thank you both.

Thanks to my sister Anne-Louise Kekic and her beautiful girls, Eva, Gabriella and Antonia, who bring much joy and happiness to the family.

I would like to thank all the people who have made this book possible. In particular, Dominic Malcolm, who supervised my Masters and PhD thesis and has been a continual source of support throughout my academic career, continuing to support my career long after the duties of a PhD supervisor were complete. Aarti: since our friendship began at Brunel University you have been a friend and academic supporter. Thanks to all my friends, who have been a source of support and provided much needed diversion from work and study.

Thank you to my colleagues and friends at YSJ, who have been a constant source of support, with special thanks to Nathalie and Anna. Finally, I would like to say a special thanks to Michelle Jones for being a supportive mentor during my time at YSJ; it has been much appreciated.

1
Introduction

Women's cricket is a global game that has had an international governing body since 1958. There are an increasing number of global competitions and at present the women's game is represented in the same national and global organisations as men's cricket, although this has not always been the case. Recently ten countries participated in the women's T20 World Cup in Bangladesh, and some female cricketers were paid to represent their countries. International tournaments and bilateral competitions are increasing and international cricket is now a year-round operation. This suggests that women cricketers are a visible, albeit marginal, part of the global game. In the introduction to *Women's Cricket and Global Processes: The Emergence and Development of Women's Cricket as a Global Game*, I start by drawing on three recent examples that highlight the changes in women's cricket as a global game, thus charting out the aims of the book and the key theoretical perspective that underpins the analysis of women's cricket as a global game.

The first example is the women's Ashes. At the time of writing this book, the England women's cricket team won the 2014 Ashes series in Australia. 'The Ashes' remain one of cricket's most prized achievements for English and Australian cricketers and the series continues to have importance and be related to ideologies of national pride and success of the 'nations', reflecting their social history and identity. The women's series has only been called the Ashes since 1998 despite matches between Australian and English women dating back to 1934, when England travelled to Australia for the first international women's cricket match. Rachael Heyhoe Flint, one of the most well-known female cricketers, describes how the women's Ashes were considered by players as being of great significance: 'The aura of the Ashes and the lure of battles against the enemies from down under outshine anything else the game can offer' (1978: 72).

The intense competition in the Ashes between the England and Australian men's teams continues to generate extensive media interest. In Australia, the Ashes symbolise a battle between the two nations that evokes images of national identity and masculinity (Stevenson, 2002). In the 2013–2014 series, the England men's team lost the series 5–0. In contrast, the England women's team won their series, and this was only the third time that this had been achieved on Australian soil. The women's Ashes is played in a format different from the men's; it is a multi-format series comprising one test match, three one-day matches and three T20 matches. The format provides six points for a test match win and two points for a win in each of the one-day and T20 formats. This variation is significant as it lessens the emphasis on the test match win and symbolises a key difference in the women's game: test match cricket remains marginal in women's cricket. The format for the women's Ashes has also often changed – for example, through the initial Ashes series, from 1934 to 1984, women played three test matches as standard; since 1984, the format has switched from five to just one test match in 2007 and 2009. For the men, the Ashes are decided through the traditional format of five test matches which has not changed throughout the history of the series.

In England, the 2013–2014 men's loss was subject to hours of media critique, with headlines such as 'England should feel ashamed and embarrassed by the Ashes defeat' (*The Telegraph*, 5 January 2014), 'Ashes whitewash was an implosion like no other in English history' (*The Telegraph*, 5 January 2014), 'Australia complete Ashes whitewash' (BBC, 5 January 2014) and 'It's a whitewash! Sorry England embarrassed by Australia after another humiliating defeat Down Under as hosts complete 5–0 rout in Sydney' (*The Daily Mail*, 5 January 2014). The focus on humiliation and the link to English history illustrates the relationship between sport and national identity. The loss of the (men's) England cricket team has often been linked to broader issues of national pride, for example, losing to India and Sri Lanka in the past has been linked to 'English Shame' (Maguire, 2012: 152). Terms such as shame and humiliation are drawn upon to indicate a broader sense of loss as a nation. Research has focused extensively on how sport can be a medium through which people identify with the nation; however, much of this research focuses on the relationship between men's sport and national identity (Mansfield and Curtis, 2009). Scholars within the sociology of sport have identified how sport is part of people's identity and specifically their national identity (Liston and Moreland, 2009), but less research has considered the relationship between gender the nation and national identity. Much research has identified how there is a strong relationship in the main cricketing nations, and the diaspora, between cricket and national identity and the recognition that cricket can reflect (or reinforce) how people think of themselves and 'others' (Malcolm, 2012). Again, this research often does not consider how women also identify with the nation through supporting (men's) cricket and to date there is no research that explores whether women's cricket reflects national pride, character and identity in the way that men's cricket does.

Women are part of the 'nation', but their sporting success does not necessarily evoke feelings of national identity in the same ways that men's sport does. The success of the England women's team in the Ashes was reported on by the media, illustrating a significant shift in gender relations in which women's sport is no longer ignored. Although this was marginal, media coverage about the women's success focused on how the women's team could restore 'national pride' after the loss of the men's team. For example, *The Telegraph* claimed that another 'English Ashes assault could not be in safer, stronger hands' (8 January 2014). The increased media attention in the women's game marks a shift in power relations between men's and women's cricket. Furthermore, while the *Telegraph* article suggests that the women's game could reflect pride and national identity, media coverage remains so slight that few people are aware of the losses or successes of the women's national team in any nation where the game is played.

Women's cricket, although developing as a global game, is not drawn upon to evoke strong feelings of national identity and pride in the way that men's cricket is. In addition, the women's game is largely dependent on the men's game for its development and support (more so since the mergers discussed in Chapters 4 and 5), especially for financial support. Women's cricket has not received much academic discussion, although the history and development of men's cricket as a national and global sport (see for example Bose,

2006; Gemmell, 2004; Majumdar, 2003; Malcolm, 2013; Nauright, 2010; Sandiford, 1998) has been subject to discussion in several academic texts. In these accounts, the women's game is largely invisible. Some establishment accounts of women's cricket exist – Joy's *Maiden Over: A Short History of Women's Cricket and a Report of the Australian Tour 1948–49* (1950), Heyhoe Flint and Rheinberg's *Fair Play: The Story of Women's Cricket* (1976) and more recently Duncan's *Skirting the Boundary: A History of Women's Cricket* (2013) – and give us some details about the history of the women's game. However, these accounts do not offer an explanation for the emergence and development of the global game, considering how social processes and power relations influence the development of women's cricket. *Women's Cricket and Global Processes: The Emergence and Development of Women's Cricket as a Global Game* therefore adopts a sociological approach to explain how and why cricket for women emerged and developed and significantly how power relations between men's and women's cricket influence the social habitus of women who play cricket.

Women's cricket: A global game

The second example also reflects a significant shift in power relations in the women's game. On 1 February 2013, the Sri Lankan women's team beat England at the World Cup during a group stage match. The importance of this win to the Sri Lankan team was highlighted by the Sri Lankan captain Shashikala Siriwardene, who described the win as the finest in her team's history: 'It's like a dream come true for us. We've been waiting for this moment for 16 years', she said. Why is beating England so important to Sri Lanka? It no doubt reflects the colonial position of cricket more broadly; beating England is associated with bringing pride to many ex-colonies, as beating the masters at their own game has an important role to play in shaping national identities and the national characters of those who follow cricket. However, what does it mean for Sri Lankans in the context of women's cricket? Acceptance? Reflection of an international standard? Undoubtedly England is at the heart of the development of women's cricket as it represents the emergence of women's cricket globally. It was the first country with a national governing body, it was at the forefront of the development of the International Women's Cricket Council (IWCC) and, having won a number of international tournaments, the England women's cricket team reflects the established group within women's cricket. Beating England demonstrates a suitable 'global' standard of play, but this emotive response by Sri Lanka indicates two key issues:

a) it further questions the role of gender, national identity and women's cricket and the extent to which women's sport can reflect national character and pride, and
b) it demonstrates the growth of the women's game and increased competitive standards of the global game, in which previous minority countries are starting to challenge and beat other 'established' teams.

Significant changes in the structure and governance of women's cricket occurred in 2005, when the women's game merged with the existing International Cricket Council (ICC). Prior to this, from 1958, women's cricket was governed by the IWCC. The merging of men's and women's cricket organisations is a trend that has also occurred in the national governance of the game. This was reinforced as part of the ICC mandate in which all countries that had separate men's and women's cricket boards had to merge the two to create one governing body that represented all elements of the game. In some instances, this mandate was enforced on national governing bodies, whereas in England, Australia and New Zealand, the mergers took place before the ICC mandate.

With the merger between the IWCC and the ICC, the women's game came under the governance of the ICC, which has a history of developing and organising the global men's game since 1909. At present, as at the time of the merger in 2005, the ICC has three membership categories – Full, Associate and Affiliate. There are ten full members of the ICC: Australia, Bangladesh, England, India, New Zealand, Pakistan, South Africa, Sri Lanka, West Indies and Zimbabwe. According to the ICC, the full membership category is for the governing bodies of cricket that are from

> a country recognised by the ICC, or nations associated for cricket purposes, or geographical area, from which representative teams are qualified to play official Test Matches. (ICC, 2013)

This definition does not mention women's cricket. Full membership is decided in relation to the status of men's cricket and more specifically test cricket. This is based on historical issues that enabled men's cricket to develop in specific ways. In women's cricket, test match cricket is rarely played, which is why the Ashes are not decided over a series of five test matches. Test match cricket has not played a significant part in the recent development of the game and some full member countries, such as Sri Lanka and Pakistan, have played less than five test matches in the last 18 years. Some of the problems associated with test match cricket for women are as follows: the length is not compatible with amateur female cricketers' schedules and the lack of competitiveness amongst some nations has meant that test match cricket has not played a significant part in the development of women's cricket, in the way it has in men's cricket. Having test match cricket status is not a reflection of standard in the women's game. Although all the full members were awarded ICC membership prior to 2005, and the merger with women's cricket, the criteria for full membership have not been reviewed and only eight of the ten full members played in the 2013 women's World Cup. Moreover, the dominance of certain teams is evident through looking at, for example, the women's World Cup. Since 1973, Australia has won six, England has won three and New Zealand has won one title.

The ten full members of the ICC and the dates on which they received full membership reflect the diffusion and development of men's cricket. Yet, the women's game has had a different trajectory of development than the men's game. As demonstrated in Table 1.1, the women's game started to follow a similar trajectory to men's cricket, but as the women's game developed, Holland and other European countries such as Ireland became influential in the women's global game. These countries went on to compete in the recent 2014 T20 World Cup. In contrast, Sri Lanka and Pakistan did not play international cricket until the 1990s. These patterns of diffusion are discussed throughout the book, specifically in Chapter 3, to consider the development of women's cricket and in discussing how these patterns may reflect broader social processes, gender relations and power.

As the table demonstrates, women's cricket does not completely mirror the development of men's cricket. The social processes involved in the development of women's cricket need to be

Table 1.1　Significant dates in the global development of men's and women's cricket

Country	Date of formation of women's national governing body	Women's national governing body joins IWCC	Men's national governing body given full membership status	Men's and women's national governing bodies merge
England	1926	1958	1909	1998
Australia	1931	1958	1909	2001
South Africa	1953	1958	1909	–
New Zealand	1934	1958	1926	2005
Holland	–	1958	–	–
West Indies	1974	1973	1926	2005
India	1973	1973	1926	2006
Ireland	–	1987	–	–
Denmark	–	1987	–	–
Sri Lanka	1999	1997	1981	–
Pakistan	1978	1997	1952	2005
Bangladesh	–	–	2000	–
Zimbabwe	–	–	1992	–

Source: IWCC, International Women's Cricket Council.

considered and explained, and this is in part the aim of *Women's Cricket and Global Processes: The Emergence and Development of Women's Cricket as a Global Game*. To do this, figurational sociology is adopted as a framework for explaining the development of women's cricket and power relations that have impacted on the emergence and continual development of women's cricket as a global game.

Women's cricket, social identities and women as outsiders in the global game

The third example says something about the women's game and the habitus or identities of those women who play the game and the response of others. On 14 January 2013, Sarah Taylor, an England cricketer, was on the front page of *The Guardian* (a British daily newspaper): the article was about her playing Second XI county cricket in the 2013 season. Nothing unusual about this you might think, other than women cricketers do not often appear on front pages of newspapers for playing cricket and this article was actually about the possibility that she might play men's cricket. In the interview in *The Guardian*, Taylor herself suggests that such a prospect is 'daunting' and that playing in the men's Second XI team, as a wicketkeeper, would be a challenge. In particular, she stresses how she would be facing a 'bigger ball and bigger bowlers' (Taylor, cited in McRae, 2013); adding to this, she needs to ask herself, 'Can you handle this?' The reference to a bigger ball and bigger bowlers is interesting as it raises the usual responses in the media discussions, drawing on ideas of men's sport being bigger, better and more of a spectacle than women's sport. These debates are not just discussed in public forums and in debates about men and women's sport, but Taylor herself questions whether she can 'handle' the men's game. Although the level that Taylor is proposing to play at in the men's game is in a men's county second team, the fact that there is so much debate about whether she has the capability to play at this level indicates how female cricketers are viewed *in comparison to male cricketers*. They are defined as weaker, both physically and psychologically. Debates about women's capabilities to play sport are often reduced to arguments about physicality and physical ability. In this respect, women are framed as biologically less suited to sport by men and women. Questions are beginning to emerge about the position of women's cricket, *in comparison to men's cricket*, and crucially about whether women's bodies are able to compete alongside male bodies. These discussions indicate that the women's game has become more 'visible' in recent years and also suggest that male and female cricketers are increasingly interdependent on one another, which may bring with it increased tensions between the two groups as the discussions about women's suitability to play cricket with men is debated. This recent example illustrates the visibility of some women who play the game and the emergence of female cricketers in the media, demonstrating a shift in power relations whilst at the same time perhaps highlighting the complexities involved in understanding the development of women's cricket in complex figurations with shifting asymmetrical power relations that continue to impact on the perceptions of female cricketers (the outsiders) in comparison to male cricketers (the established).

A theoretical framework for understanding gender relations and cricket

The adoption of figurational sociology to understanding gender relations may seem unusual given the extensive debates about whether the theory is suitable for understanding issues of gender relations (Hargreaves, 1992, 1994). In this book, figurational sociology is used as a sensitising framework to explain the emergence and development of women's cricket and how wider social processes influenced the game, to explain the emergence of women's cricket in different contexts and to consider how power relations constrain and enable the development of the game, as well as to consider the identities of the women who play the global game.

Given the centrality of Elias' work on civilising processes in the sociology of sport, it is largely this aspect of his work that has been applied in the field and as a consequence of this figurational sociology has become synonymous to most as being solely related to civilising processes (often considered to focus just on violence within sport), with other elements of Elias' work being marginalised or less understood or applied in this field. For example, figurational sociology has been applied to understanding the emergence and development of modern sports, including, but not limited to, football and football-related violence, cricket (Malcolm, 2004, 2013), boxing (Sheard, 2004), tennis (Cooper, 2004; Lake, 2009), motor racing (Twitchen, 2004) and gymnastics (Benn and Benn, 2004). Such accounts have courted much criticism and in particular Hargreaves (1992) is right to point out that many figurational studies have 'concentrated on male sports or male bonding'. In an attempt to counter this, more recent studies such as those by Maguire and Mansfield (1998), Mansfield (2002, 2008) and Liston (2005, 2006, 2014) have argued that figurational sociology can be adopted to explore gender relations in sport. Despite these accounts, Hargreaves' critique that 'the figurational approach is markedly masculinist' (Hargreaves, 1992: 161) has meant that an ongoing perception within sociology of sport is that figurational sociology does not and cannot offer an adequate understanding of gender relations in sport. Whilst acknowledging these critiques and counter-critiques, which I do not intend to repeat here, it is my contention – throughout my academic work to date, on a range of female experiences of male sport – that figurational sociology can offer an analysis of gender relations of sport. Not that this is or should be the only analysis but that my application of the theoretical concepts of Eliasian sociology have enabled a sociological analysis of gender relations in cricket that will be adopted throughout this book. In particular, Mansfield (2008: 95) summarises the central tenets of Elias' work as being committed to the development of

> several arguments connected to the role of the state in social development, science as a social institution, the inextricable relationship between social development (sociogenesis) and developments in personality structures (psychogenesis) and power relations in terms of tensions between established and outsider groups.

In essence, this quote captures the key aspects of analysis adopted in this text as a study of the changes in social development and personality structures between established and outsider groups, drawing on long-term social processes to consider how power imbalances change through a variety of social processes.

One of the central concepts of figurational sociology is the figuration itself which is utilised as a processual term that captures the interdependent relationships that people are part of and how these relate to one another. The term figuration offers a way of understanding how people are part of complex interdependencies and as part of interdependent processes there are unintended consequences that develop from social processes and relations. As Malcolm (2013: 168) describes, 'Human interdependence works like re-bounding ripples in a pond, intermingling in multiple, complex and unanticipated ways'. The term figuration captures the interdependency of humans and the power balances that exist within such relations. The concept of the figuration, which moves away from static ideas about human relationships and macro- and micro-structures, allows for an analysis of complex power relations between groups that have varying degrees of interdependency. Sometimes people are aware of the figurations in which they are involved, but other figurations where people are dependent on others are less evident in people's everyday lives: for example, global processes and the interdependent relations that people are involved in are less evident but can impact on people's lives, experiences and identities.

Civilising processes and gender relations

The focus of Elias' *The Civilising Process*, his central theory, is to demonstrate long-term changes in people's behaviour and emotions which coincide with a change in wider social changes such as state formation (Dunning and Hughes, 2013). *The Civilising Process* outlines a central theory which stresses the importance of creating theories based on empirical observations that are applicable to the lives of people and to create knowledge (Elias, 1978). Whilst sometimes critiqued as a passing of value judgements on civilised behaviour, this is not the case as the text considers the ways in which people came to view themselves as more civilised than others. Thus, it is not about the moral elements of what constitutes civilised people, but more about how social life has become more regulated, through the internalisation of external social controls (Malcolm, 2013).

Elias demonstrated how standards of behaviour and psychological make-up have changed in Europe since the Middle Ages, focusing on complex social processes which enabled these standards of behaviour to change. The strength of this approach is that Elias links long-term structural developments in societies with long-term changes in people's habitus (Dunning and Hughes, 2013). Concomitant changes in personality begin with elite groups and then are gradually dispersed to other groups. The reason for these changes can be explained through the increasing social interdependencies between groups, as groups are forced to pay more attention to one another. As part of these processes, the balance of control between individuals shifts from external constraints to more internalised self-constraint. Although it is widely considered that Elias did not mention gender relations in *The Civilising Process*, this is not entirely true. Elias did mention gender relations, albeit not extensively. Like all relations between groups, Elias insists on considering how gender relations impact on men and women, both from a psychogenesis as well as a sociogenesis perspective and to consider how these relations have changed over long periods of time. One example that Elias draws upon that relates to gender relations and changing relations between the sexes in *The Civilising Process* is how changes in relations over time require greater internal restraint on the part of men and women over sexual desires. For instance, Elias notes that in the 19th century, concern over women wearing bathing costumes was focused on concern about men's lack of sexual control, yet in modern societies, bathing costumes show the female body; this demonstrates a high standard of control where sexual restraint is taken for granted, and although a simple description, this demonstrates a clear civilising direction in relation to sexuality. For example, the gradual removal of sexuality to behind the scenes and advancing thresholds of shame and embarrassment, greater mutual identification between men and women, and a shift in the balance between external control and self-control are evident in relation to sexuality (Mennell, 1992). The intervention of the state in marriage and divorce is a further example of changes in relations between the sexes, and state intervention is critical in the reduction of power relations as it can enforce judgements in the balance of power between men and women.

Advancing the work of Elias and focusing on gender relations and long-term social processes, Brinkgreve (2004) illustrates that in Western countries, power relations between the sexes have changed. She identified key time periods in accelerating or reinforcing power imbalances. Through the monopolisation of three resources – physical strength, knowledge and organisation – Brinkgreve (2004) suggests that men manage to acquire 'superior power positions' which 'leans towards the advantage of males' (Brinkgreve 2004: 142). Through tracing long-term social processes, Brinkgreve (2004) illustrates that these power resources have been reduced and power ratios have changed, for example economic dependence on men has decreased through women's entry into the workplace and the rise of the welfare state which enabled women to access state support to raise families and which ensures women are not entirely dependent on men for economic support. Other changes such as increase in technological advances and contraception have enabled women greater entry into public spheres. Other state interventions, such as the monopoly on violence, are critical as it has become illegal for men to be violent towards women. That is not to say that violence has been eradicated, but it could be argued that it is increasingly considered to be repugnant to be violent to women and the state can punish individuals convicted of violence (Mierzwinski et al., 2014). Such changes require new levels of internal restraint and changes in the psyches of men and women.

Changes in relations between the sexes reveal changes at the level of psychogenesis and sociogenesis, just as changes in the job market from an industrial to service economy industry, alongside changes in law and education, brought differing standards of emotional control from men and women, and suggest some difference in the expectations of civilising female and male bodies (Mierzwinski et al., 2014). For example, men have to be increasingly more empathetic in considering the views and needs of women. Through taking a long-term perspective on gender relations, a trend towards equalisation is evident. Furthermore, these processes are not linear, not without tensions, and changes have 'not penetrated all social groups as an ideal, let alone a form of practice' (Brinkgreve, 2004: 148). Gender relations are complex and like all relations within civilising processes they can be reversed under particular conditions. In another paper, Brinkgreve (2003) discusses relations between the sexes in relation to changes in the demands of relationships, and she notes that increased mutual identification through greater levels of interdependency has led to greater expectations between partners. This is no less constraining than previous relations and brings with it other demands that expect greater levels of mutual restraint (Brinkgreve, 2003).

Providing a processual understanding of the development of women's cricket in relation to the development of the global men's game is critical in utilising a figurational analysis of how the relationship between men's cricket and other social processes such as nationalism, diffusion, colonialism and masculinity impacts on the development of women's cricket. This focus on relational power is a key part of the analysis presented in this book, as one of the premises adopted is to explain how and why the women's game emerged in different contexts and how gender relations and the emergence of complex established and outsider figurations influenced and continue to influence the development of the women's game.

Cricket and civilising processes

The application of the concepts of civilising processes to understanding the development of men's cricket and the relationship between cricket and civilising processes is fairly well documented (Malcolm, 2002, 2013). At the time of its diffusion, cricket was used in some colonial contexts as a sport that could 'civilise' what were perceived as uncivilised indigenous populations. The codification of cricket is central to the diffusion process at a time when cricket was most strongly linked to ideological notions of Englishness and nationality (and masculinity) (Malcolm, 2013). It is important not to oversimplify the diffusion of cricket as it was not a linear process. There have been different degrees of adoption, adaptation and resistance in men's cricket and diffusion involves complex social processes and power relations that have been discussed elsewhere (see Malcolm, 2013).

Cricket is frequently described as an Imperial Game and as a reflection of this the first governing body of men's cricket was called the Imperial Cricket Council. The imperial council was founded in 1909 by England, Australia and South Africa and, until the 1990s, the president of the council was the same as that of the Marylebone Cricket Club (MCC), reflecting the dominance of England in the broader development of the game. Australia and England also had veto powers in the organisation of the men's game until the 1990s and were strongly able to influence the development of men's cricket to shape the development of cricket in ways that suited these two nations. It was only in 1989 that the organisation changed its name to the International Cricket Council, reflecting a change in the global game to a more inclusive structure. Since then, power relations in the men's game have arguably changed significantly and the development of cricket has largely been driven by the commercial developments in the game and the shift in power relations that have enabled changes in the game, for example, the increase in T20 cricket and the emergence of the Indian Premier League (IPL).

Cricket was utilised to varying degrees in the Empire as a sport that reflected civilised elements of Englishness and identity. The British took a positive self-image from their involvement in the Empire, viewing their dominance as a reflection of their supremacy and intelligence. In light of the dominance of social Darwinism as an ideology, there was a view that the colonisers were superior and had characteristics that were not possessed by indigenous populations, and therefore colonialism was viewed as natural and inevitable. Cricket was important in discussions about civilising others as it was a game that reflected English rural life. The game was popular in English public schools as it was believed to teach boys values that would enable them to become imperial administrators and leaders (Williams, 2001). Cricket was viewed as a civilising mission and discussions about the levels of violence in the game and where the game is played have continued throughout its development. Often discussions about how 'others' play the game has focused on ideas about violence and different levels of violence in different nation states. This emphasis on violence had the effect of presenting other cultures as uncivilised and arguing that, for instance, bowling styles, or match fixing, are reflective of cultural issues that are indigenous to others. According to Elias, the very concept of civilisation forms parts of Western self-consciousness and is often an expression of national identities. The fact that some people view themselves as more civilised than others is evident in the self-conception of the personalities of people in Western societies, a view that is seen in the 'othering' of communities or cultures that are presented as needing Western intervention. Cricket encapsulated the view of British civilised (gentlemen), as Appadurai (1996: 93) notes

> Cricket was seen as an ideal way to socialise natives [who were perceived as lazy, enervated, and effect] into new modes of inter-group conduct and new standards of public behaviour.

As outlined in Chapter 2, interdependency is central to a figurational understanding of the diffusion of cricket and colonialism more broadly. Levels of interdependency between groups are important to consider, especially during radical changes, and unintended consequences are evident in the history and development of men's and *women's* cricket, although much less is known about the latter. Little is known about the relationship between men's and women's cricket; other research on women and civilising processes highlights how women are often considered to have a civilising influence (Thing, 2001). This view is based on the notion that women are less aggressive and more passive than men, but this is not a biological characteristic of being a woman but more a reflection of a type of civilising process in which male and female bodies and behaviour codes/expectations may have differed through Western civilising process, suggesting a distinctly gendered civilising process. In Chapter 3, I adopt some concepts of civilising processes to consider the emergence, formation and development of women's cricket in nation states, considering the differing levels of acceptance of and resistance to women's cricket across the globe.

The theory of established and outsider relations

Elias rejected contemporary sociological concepts of power by rejecting power as a 'thing' that one possesses. Instead, he argues that power is part of all relationships and should be viewed as a balance and as relational. Power is a part of the interdependent relationships that all people are involved in. The theory of established and outsiders is linked to civilising processes as both explore 'changing power relations between groups (and) the social habitus of group members' (Mennell, 1992). In Elias' joint work with Scotson (1994), they demonstrate the use of established and outsider relations to understanding how one group in a community was subordinate to another group. Of particular interest was that both groups were similar in relation to conventional measures of social stratification, occupation and wealth. The authors consider how the established group is able to monopolise local resources and networks of gossip. This group is able to do this through their levels of cohesion and networks of interdependencies. Gossip is used as a dual process by which one group elevates its own social position while at the same time encouraging others to see the other group as badly behaved, unclean and *uncivilised*. Thus, the dual process of group charisma and group disgrace enables one group to view the others as different and inferior: 'There is one image tended towards denigration and the other towards idealization' (Mennell, 1992: 119).

One of the key elements of understanding the interdependence between the established and outsiders is how the outsiders begin to internalise their group disgrace, often identifying with the established group; this considers how the social habitus and personality of groups is affected by broader social process. The process of stigmatising one group demonstrates the socio-dynamics of stigmatisation and is linked closely to identity, as 'exclusion and stigmatisation of the outsiders by the established group, were two powerful weapons used by the latter to maintain their identity' (Malcolm and Velija, 2008: 4). Stigmatisation can take many forms, but crucially, it is socially created through processes such as blame gossip, which can form a powerful view of the outsider group by the established.

The theory of established and outsider relations can be used to explore relations between groups in different contexts as there are characteristics that can be applied to all established and outsider relations. These are the establishment of I/we/they images that emphasise superiority, the development and enforcement of exclusion strategies and the stigmatisation of the less-powerful group (Maguire, 1999). Power between the established and the outsider may be very marked or may be moving towards equalisation, and when power balances are changing, the sense of inferiority that is felt by the outsiders may be challenged. The shifting change in power balances between groups is captured in the term *functional democratisation*. This term represents a process of social transformation of power relations between groups through denser webs of interdependence (Dunning and Hughes, 2013). Functional democratisation occurs through the greater reciprocal dependence between groups and social function between groups leads towards *diminishing contrasts and increasing varieties* (Mennell, 1992: 109). When utilising the concepts of established and outsider relations as a framework, and as a sensitising framework for exploring power relations between groups, Mennell (1992) suggests considering the following:

- How interdependent are the two groups and how far are power relations titled in the groups? Are these stable or fluctuating?
- How is one group able to monopolise something the other side needs?
- What is the process of stigmatisation and operation of group charisma and group disgrace?
- Where the balance of power is becoming more equal, consider aspects of rebellion, resistance and emancipation amongst the outsiders; a long-term perspective to relations is needed here.
- How realistic are the images that the groups have of one another is also of interest; Elias suggests that the more unequal the power balance, the less realistic and more fantasy-laden the image of the outsiders on the part of the established.

The theory of established and outsider relations is utilised in Chapters 3 and 5 as a framework for understanding power relations in women's cricket. Established and outsider relations in women's cricket are complex and within global cricket figurations established and outsider relations figurations exist between cricketing nations. For example, within international governing bodies, arguably women cricketers are outsiders, yet within women's cricket, there are power relations between cricketing nations that have historically influenced the development of women's cricket in particular ways. More broadly the acceptance and resistance to women's cricket is complex, in flux, and it is critical to understand the social processes involved in the emergence and development of the game and in particular the emergence of established and outsider relations in the development of cricket as a modern sport.

Gender and global processes in sport

A figurational approach to understanding global processes in sport differs from other theories of globalisation and global sport (Dunning, 1999). Whilst a figurational analysis does not deny economics in understanding global processes, a figurational approach focuses on broader processes that are considered equally important in understanding these developments (Dunning, 1999). In providing a figurational analysis of global sport, Maguire (2011) draws on figurational sociology as a framework for understanding global processes in sport, suggests that utilising Eliasian concepts are fruitful in understanding global sport processes as they can probe networks of power balances and interdependencies, and highlights the occidental practice of using civilised behaviour as a marker of prestige and the attention given to the dynamics of established and outsider relations. As Maguire (2011) highlights, several competing theories exist in globalisation research such as modernisation perspectives, theories of imperialism, dependency theory, world system theory and globalisation research. A figurational approach to globalisation focuses on rejecting monocausal logic evident in some accounts and considers the balance between intended and unintended outcomes that no economic, political or ideological processes are able to control. There are unintended outcomes of such social processes that emerge out of interdependent processes which no one person can plan. For example, in cricket, no one person could have intended for cricket to have been adopted so comprehensively in India. As Ashis Nandy (cited in Malcolm et al., 2009: 432) famously said, 'Cricket is an Indian game, invented accidentally by the English' – the adoption and acceptance of cricket as an Indian sport, and a national sport, is not the result of an intended outcome, but rather this is the result of a set of social processes and interdependent relations that have intended and unintended consequences (Malcolm, 2013). Maguire (2005) suggests that game models are useful for understanding global processes as they explain the interdependence and power of the processes and consider how out-of-intended processes beget unintended consequences. Global processes are not a recent phenomenon but are long term in nature; global flows and rate of change may accelerate at specific times and leisure styles/sports are examples of processes. As part of globalisation processes, interdependency between groups increased; this can be seen in the global economy, for example, where the West has become more dependent on others for goods and this has meant that interdependence among nations has increased. Contact between people, and among groups, has increased and people are able to travel or communicate with others at great distance with ease. Global processes do not, however, lead to homogeneity as within these relations there can be a reinforcement of local/national and global identities (Maguire, 2011). Such processes cannot be reduced to single causal factors, although what is clear here is that within such processes are related to ideological practices.

However, within these relations, there also exist complex established and outsider relations and established groups are able to organise a positive 'we' identity whilst also controlling aspects of a negative image of the outsider group. The processes of stigmatisation mean that it can be difficult for outsider groups to resist the established group's view of the outsiders and stigma is deeply embedded in the personality of the outsider group. That is not to say that such relations are static, but that they are in flux and that outsider groups are certainly not powerless, but even at the level of individual habitus, outsider groups may internalise the views of the established group. In the diffusion and development of sport, there are several relations between groups and shifting power balances, as Maguire (1999) stresses how, within these relations, 'power, culture, and control are at the heart of global sport processes'. The majority of research about global processes in sport have focused on men, and even more broadly, a criticism of globalisation research is the way it has ignored gender relations (Wolfe, 1991). Another key aspect of research on global flows focuses on male labour migration (Elliot and Maguire, 2008; Maguire, 1993). Male labour migration is of course gendered, as it is women who facilitate these moves through their performance of domestic labour and childcare, supporting their husbands in their sporting careers. Despite the focus on global flows in male sport, recent evidence suggests that women do migrate for sporting reasons although this is rarely for financial gain: 'In the case of soccer migration, we see global exchange developing even if the money is very modest and the media attention low' (Botelho and Agergarrd, 2011: 817). Little research has explored the experiences of women who are involved in labour sport migration; in women's cricket, there is a long established history of women experiencing labour sport migration, although this is rarely for financial gain, as discussed in Chapter 5.

The aims of this book

Underpinning the analysis in this text are specific principles drawn from figurational sociology. These focus on power relations between groups and long-term social processes. Essentially, the aim of the book is to make women's cricket visible and to readdress the balance of academic research in cricket, which has predominantly focused on men's cricket. To understand the current position of women's cricket, it is necessary to understand its historical and social context. A sociological analysis of the women's game as a global game is currently absent in the academic literature and at the core of this text are the following sociological questions:

- How have civilising processes enabled and constrained the development of women's cricket in different national contexts?
- What social processes were involved in the emergence and development of men's cricket nationally and internationally and how established and outsider figurations that developed between men and women were created in national and international contexts?
- What social processes have enabled and constrained the development of women's cricket, nationally and internationally?
- How do shifting mutual power balances between men and women in cricket impact on the development of the game?

These questions are critical for understanding *and explaining* the development of women's cricket and the current global game.

   The book is not about men's cricket and whilst men's cricket is discussed as a way of understanding the relations between men's and women's cricket, the focus is not to repeat previous histories of men's cricket, but where necessary, explain how established and outsider relations developed in cricket, locating the women's game in the broader context of other social processes such as diffusion and post-colonialism that have inevitably influenced the development of women's cricket. The data used in this book have been collected over a 13-year period of researching women's cricket. These include records from annuals and year books from the England Women's Cricket Association and IWCC, establishment accounts of the women's game, interviews with women cricketers in the United Kingdom, interviews with players across the globe and interviews with women who were involved in the structure and organisation of women's cricket prior to the merger of women's cricket with men's cricket.

The aim of the book is to develop a sociological, more specifically a figurational, understanding of the social processes that have shaped the emergence and development of women's cricket as a global game. Chapter 2 begins by outlining the emergence of cricket in England as a modern sport, exploring in particular the dual processes of sportisation and parliamentarisation considering how established and outsider figuration between men and women's cricket emerged, especially focusing on the under-researched aspect of considering the relationship between cricket, nationality and masculinity in England. As a comparison, this chapter also considers the emergence of women's cricket in Australia, looking at the diffusion of cricket to Australia, its role in broader debates about colonialism and colonial power, and how the women's game emerged in this social context with resistance to women playing a 'male sport', again drawing on the theory of established and outsider relations to understand how the game developed in relation to broader issues of gender relations. This chapter finishes by identifying the emergence of women's cricket as an international sport by 1934 during the first international tour between England and Australia, signalling the emergence of international women's cricket.

Chapter 3 draws on key aspects of civilising processes, functional democratisation and established and outsider relations to explore the emergence of men's and women's cricket in a variety of different global nations. This includes several of the full members of the ICC, including India, Pakistan, New Zealand, Sri Lanka and the West Indies, and the more marginal nations such as Ireland and Holland in which the women's game has developed, but cricket more broadly is not popular in these nations. This analysis considers when cricket was diffused and how such patterns of diffusion and the relationship between cricket, masculinity and nationality influence the emergence and development of women's cricket. Given that cricket is played in eight of the ten full member countries of the ICC, the varying degrees of support given to women's cricket has meant that the women's game has developed at a different pace and pattern to men's cricket, and I draw on sensitising concepts from the civilising processes to offer an explanation for how the development of women's cricket in different nation states may be related to broader social processes and power relations between the sexes.

Chapter 4 focuses on global issues in the structure and organisation of women's cricket. The chapter starts with consideration of the emergence of the IWCC in 1958 to the merger with the ICC in 2005. In parallel, the development of the 1973 and subsequent World Cups for women is considered. In this chapter, the merger of men's and women's cricket organisations in England and Australia is discussed, with specific focus on wider gender relations that enable such mergers to take place, especially considering how mergers can be both enabling and constraining for the women's game. In doing so, shifting mutual power balances are discussed in relation to the increasing interdependency between male and female cricketers and how these relations impact on established and outsider groups and increased interdependency enables a power resource for female cricketers.

Chapter 5, building on Chapter 4, draws on data from elite women cricketers who play cricket for their respective countries across several different nations. Providing an analysis that draws on interview data with the experiences of women cricketers across the globe, this chapter considers how established and outsider relations impact on the social habitus of the outsider group. It focuses on women's experiences within different cricketing nations that play the game and how these relations are affected by established and outsider relations which are in flux, with interdependency ties increasing between men and women cricketers globally and organisationally. It also explores how social identities are formed and impacted on by wider social processes. The final section in this chapter considers the experiences of the committee involved in the England Women's Cricket Association through the merger with the men's England and Wales Cricket Board, looking at the social processes involved in such mergers, thinking specifically about how such organisational changes may influence or impact on the social habitus of those involved.

In concluding *Women's Cricket and Global Processes: The Emergence and Development of Women's Cricket as a Global Game,* I reflect on the use of figurational sociology as a framework for the analysis of gender relations and consider some current issues in the women's global game considering how exploring issues through long-term social processes can enable us to understand complex global women's sport and gender relations more broadly.

2
Cricket and Masculinity in Early Forms of Cricket

Cricket developed as a modern sport in England and it was in England that the first 'laws' of the game were published. The first recorded women's match was also played in England in 1745. The first country to have a governing body for the women's game was also England, in 1926. Whilst a substantial amount has been written about the men's game and the history, development and diffusion of the game, far less is understood about the women's game from its initial development and the social processes that enabled the game to develop as a global sport. The women's game and its development need to be considered in relation to the development of men's cricket. One of the specific focuses of Eliasian sociology is to consider the relational aspect of power relations; given this context, Chapter 2 seeks to explore the emergence of cricket as a modern sport in England and its association with Englishness and masculinity, which is critical for understanding the development of the women's game.

Drawing on the framework of the theory of established and outsider relations, I consider how the established and outsider figuration between male and female cricketers emerged in English and Australian cricket, considering how processes enabled and constrained the development of women's cricket in two different contexts. For example, exploring how, in the Australian context, the diffusion of sport is associated with national and masculine identities that constrained the development of women's cricket, which went through stages of vast development and then decline until the formation of the Australian Women's Cricket Council (AWCC), which brought some stability to the development of cricket for women and girls in Australia.

This chapter is not meant to be an exhaustive historical account of the development of cricket in England and Australia. Instead, it focuses on the processes that enabled cricket to emerge as a male preserve and the subsequent characteristics of established and outsider figurations in two different contexts, focusing on how the identities of those involved in these figurations are interlinked and comprise the key characteristics of established and outsider figurations. I start by exploring the emergence and development of cricket as a modern sport and how the social processes involved influenced the development of women's cricket.

English folk games, cricket and gender

Early forms of cricket were played as folk games of various forms and with differing rules (Malcolm, 2013). Evidence suggests women were involved in playing folk games at this time and were involved in a number of sporting activities; these activities were different depending on class, but it is often a misconception that women were not involved in early forms of folk games (Guttmann, 1991). The first-recorded women's cricket match was played in England in 1745. The match was mentioned in *The Reading Mercury* on 26 July 1745 and was described as 'the greatest cricket-match that ever was played in south part of England' (Heyhoe Flint and Rheinberg 1976: 14). Around this time, it seems that women's cricket teams were often made up of married vs single women and post matches there was dance, tea and ale. These matches would bear little resemblance to cricket today; at this time the game had few rules and what rules existed were localised and not standardised. Men's cricket at this time did not represent the romantic view of cricket that people now have. Men's cricket matches were frequently reported as being violent and disordered, and injury and death of players was fairly commonplace, and whilst deaths were viewed as unfortunate, there was no extensive concern (Malcolm, 2012).

Women's behaviour at early matches was reported as being 'rowdy', and during one women's match in 1833, it was reported:

> As well as frequent applications to the tankard, they rendered themselves objects such as no husband, brother, parent or lover could contemplate with any degree of satisfaction. (cited in Heyhoe Flint and Rheinberg, 1976: 20)

These comments, focusing on women's behaviour and how it would be viewed by men, suggest that behavioural codes were significantly different for men and women and that such behavioural codes were decided by males. The behaviour displayed by women at the match was viewed as *uncivilised* by males and some females, and the view was that women with such wayward behaviour would not be suitable as wives or mothers. Later cricketers also viewed these women with disdain; for example, in 1950, Joy, an England cricketer writing about her 1948–49 Australian tour, mentions this quote above and, judging the behaviour of previous cricketers, prefaces it with 'we brace ourselves to print this extract *in extenso,* but we put it last, to show what we think of them' (1950: 22). Even in the 1950s, women cricketers considered this behaviour inappropriate, which demonstrates the need for women to apply behavioural restraint in ways not necessarily expected of men.

Another type of cricket was played at this time by 'ladies' at private grounds and houses. These matches were supported by notable males; for instance, in a *lady's and gentleman's magazine* in 1777 the Duke of Dorset wrote, 'What is human life but a game of cricket? And if so, why should not the ladies play it as well as we?' (cited in Heyhoe Flint and Rheinberg, 1976). Cricket for ladies was generally supported by some gentlemen. In these matches, feminine codes of behaviour were strictly adhered to; women wore ladies' clothing which was restrictive, but feminine, and they were not taken seriously as players. Nevertheless they were encouraged to get involved, under conditions which ensured propriety and femininity.

During these early days it is evident that women played cricket, and were not physically prevented from doing so, although the extent to which women played is not really fully documented; moreover, those women who did play were not necessarily taken seriously and there were behavioural codes expected of women playing (Guttman, 1991). At this time there were distinct differences in women's participation as dictated by class relations. There were also differences with regard to expected feminine behaviours, which were considered to be different for women from different social classes. Social Class was an important distinction in how women were able to access opportunities for leisure and sport. Despite these examples of women playing cricket, it is unlikely that women played as extensively or as frequently as men did. Cricket was largely viewed as a male sport as it underwent significant changes through the processes of parliamentarisation and sportisation; in the 1800s, women's access to the game became even more limited.

Parliamentarisation and sportisation

Sportisation is the term used by figurational sociologists to describe the processes involved in the transformation of violent pastimes into modern day sports (Elias and Dunning, 1986). It is used alongside the term 'parliamentarisation'. Parliament emerged in the 18th century as an organisation where disputing groups were forced to settle disagreements and conflict without violence. Such a shift required a behavioural change amongst the aristocracy and greater restraint. This was concomitant with a reduction in violence in society. As violence was increasingly frowned upon in everyday life, the enjoyment of violent pastimes was considered barbaric and it was in this context that modern sport developed (Dunning, 1999). The relationship between sportisation and parliamentarisation is not viewed as causal, but rather they are processes that occurred roughly at the same time;

> Military skills gave way to verbal skills of debate. Crucial in both these parliamentarization and sportization processes was the involvement of the landed aristocracy and gentry. This perspective does not argue that parliamentarization caused sportization, still less that the sportization of pastimes caused the parliamentarization of politics (Jarvie and Maguire, 1994: 140).

As part of these dual processes, the shift towards greater restraint and peaceful settlement of disputes was increasingly valued (Malcolm, 2012).

Cricket was the first team sport to undergo changes related to sportisation and the central actors in adapting cricket into a modern sport were parliamentarians meeting at a member's club (Malcolm, 2012). The involvement of members of parliament in the game is discussed by Malcolm (2012). The dual processes of parliamentarisation and sportisation are not characterised as being gendered, yet both processes predominantly involved men and this is significant in understanding broader gender relations in the formation of nation states. It was men, as part of parliament, who made decisions about economics, politics, education, and family and social life; thus power relations between men and women at this time were extremely unbalanced. Parliamentarisation was a process monopolised by men, and the concomitant process of sportisation meant that modern sport forms largely reflected the behavioural codes of men (although there were class differences). The first cricket rules were called 'laws of the game', the term 'laws' here, rather than 'rules', demonstrates a link between parliament and cricket, further reflecting the personalities of those involved in creating them. The first organising body for cricket was the MCC, formed in 1787, a male-only club made up of the members of the existing White Conduit Club (Malcolm, 2013).

From the outset, the club was a male preserve and this continued throughout the history of the game; a male preserve is described as a 'social institution honoured, demarcated and dominated both organizationally and ideologically by males' (Mansfield, 2002). The most significant standardisation of cricket, according to Malcolm (2002), occurred prior to the formation of the MCC in 1755 when there was an attempt to outline how batsmen could be dismissed and these laws reduced the likelihood of injury. Furthermore the introduction of an umpire into the game to uphold rules was significant as it introduced the element of a third party, separate from the game, to preside over the laws. These changes to the existing laws reduced the likelihood of violence and injury, but this was not necessarily a conscious and explicit attempt; rather, in the creation of rules there was a pattern

> so distinct that clarification and standardisation of a range of rules can most adequately be conceived as indicative of the broader, more deep rooted social change (Malcolm, 2005: 116).

Through such social processes cricket became a more 'civilised modern sport' that reflected the needs of the group involved in the game and also reflected their identities, that is, it largely represented the interests of male social elites (Parry and Malcolm, 2004). As Malcolm (2012: 29) argues, the link between parliament and cricket was particularly pronounced as cricket came to 'embody the character traits which the English regarded as the source of their distinctive and distinguished status'. Masculinity and, more specifically, discourses about a type of masculinity became firmly rooted in the development of cricket as a modern sport form and this is significant when we consider women's involvement in cricket.

Through these processes cricket became increasingly associated with a sense of English national identity and at this time women's participation declined (Malcolm, 2012). The broader processes of the development of nation states are significant here, as both the nation state and the activities associated with national identity are arguably gendered: 'State power emerged a male power and has become an organized and institutionalized form of social dominance' (Hargreaves, 1994). The state represented a form of male power; as Brinkgreve (2004) argues, male power as part of the state is significant in understanding power relations between men and women and is an example of how established groups monopolise key resources such as laws, finances and education. Cricket was strongly viewed as an English sport – one that represented English identities – and in order to be strongly identified as such, arguably it had to exclude foreigners and women. In this respect increasingly the sport became promoted as a 'nationalistic cult of masculinity' (Malcolm and Velija, 2008: 220).

19th-century cricket: The emergence of established and outsider figurations

The 19th century saw key changes in the development of the men's game and these were related to a reduction in violent play, codification and crowds becoming more orderly. The relationship between cricket and national identity strengthened as cricket came to represent a 'national sport'. Malcolm (2012) suggests that the relationship between Englishness and cricket is so developed because the histories of both are so entwined. Cricket representation also changed in the latter part of the 18th century in line with the changing relationship between the bourgeoisie and aristocracy, and the emergence of a new literary class was increasingly able to shape and define national identity. National identity was formed around the notion that Englishmen were considered to be honest, frank and moral, virtues that were believed to be proved through involvement in cricket. The focus continued to be on national identity and men, although it is likely that women also valued these attributes in gentlemen, especially when looking to marry. Literature at this time reflects the relationship between cricket and national identity; for example, in the introduction to *Cricketers of My Time,* the author described the characteristics of good cricketers as follows: 'The good cricketer will of course be a man' (cited in Malcolm, 2013: 235). The relationship between cricket and masculinity is so firmly established in the game and the literature around the game that cricket and moral worth are synonymous with masculinity. An increasing amount of literature about cricket reflected a self-conception of English people as being 'civilised'. In a similar way to the connection between sportisation and parliamentarisation, there were concomitant processes in the relationship between English national character and cricket as a national game. In 19th-century literature, cricket is also described nostalgically and links the game to village life, to an inclusive and community game, ignoring the violent history of the game. In fact, 19th-century cricket romanticises the game and often ignores the continuing dangers of the game relating to injury and rejects its elitist and violent past. In the 19th century changes to the laws of the game included the legalisation of overarm bowling and the increase in cricket professionals. During this time power relations between the MCC and others involved in the game reduced and broader changes included the number of seats in the House of Lords being increased to allow for more representation by a new male middle class. This change in cricket can be seen in the composition of members in the MCC, as in 1833 only 25 of the 202 MCC members had titles. Changes in the game's laws were frequent and as an unintended consequence the roles between players became more distinct. Yet, in many ways, it was not until 1864 that cricket began to reflect the game's modern character (Brookes, 1978).

By the end of the 19th century, the game saw more changes in governance and commercialisation. From the 1890s onwards, the game entered a golden age as pitches improved and injuries occurred less often through the introduction of protector equipment, another key element of civilising processes. Crowds became much more orderly although there continued to be examples of disorder. At this time there was a shift from the domestic game to the imperial game and arguably this further cemented the relationship between cricket and masculinity.

English cricket, gender and overarm bowling

At a time when women's involvement in cricket was at its lowest, a major development in the men's game at the start of the 19th century – overarm bowling – is attributed to a woman who is thought to have designed this action. Overarm bowling was introduced amidst controversy and reflects in part the class struggles about the game and concern about the game going into decline. Overarm bowling was introduced by John Willes in the 1820s and it caused controversy (Malcolm, 2012). The 'story' about how overarm bowling was invented is commonly attributed to John Willes's sister: when bowling underarm to her brother, her skirt was in the way and she bowled overarm instead; her brother copied this action (Duncan, 2013). Other variations of the story attribute the action to W. G. Grace's mother and some others to the daughters of William Lilywhite (McCrone, 1988). In all these stories overarm bowling is attributed to a woman, and in the establishment history of the game, women's role in the invention of overarm bowling is recounted as a popular sporting myth that seems to ratify women's role in the game. However, as argued elsewhere in Malcolm and Velija (2008), it is unlikely that women invented the overarm bowling action. Instead we offer a different explanation for why the action may be attributed to a woman. At the time of its introduction overarm bowling was discredited by the cricket establishment, and there was a view suggesting that the technique was less than manly. By attributing the action to a woman, this ridiculed the action even further, proving that the action was unmanly, similar to the way in which 'throwing like a girl' is used as a derogatory term which suggests that women's ability to throw is less than men's ability to throw, drawing on long-term ideologies about men's and women's bodies which portray women's bodies as being weaker than men's. The notion of overarm bowling being invented by women is unlikely at this time, and rather suggests the use of language and ridicule towards a new action that was not viewed as being suitable for cricket.

'Neither ladies nor cricketers': Women's cricket in England in the 19th century

Despite reports of women playing cricket from 1745, between 1840 and 1860 little discussion of the women's game exists, suggesting a decline in women playing the game. This is significant as the men's game was developing rules that focused on codifying the game and developing it as a popular game that reflected English male national identity and women's involvement in the game was marginalised. Put simply, cricket as a modern sport was developed by men for men, reflective of broader gender relations at this time; women's involvement was either marginalised or, in the case of the organisation of the game, ignored.

Women's cricket seems to re-emerge with the girls' public schools; for example, girls playing cricket is mentioned at a ladies' school near Frome (McCrone, 1988). Other schools, such as St Leonards School in St Andrews, Girton College in Cambridge, and Roedean School, introduced the sport for girls. At Roedean School, Penelope Lawrence gave the following justification for girls playing: 'A strong social bond between the mother country and the colonies, between class and class, and race and race' (cited in Guttmann, 1991: 108). By 1897 there were eight cricket teams at Roedean School (Duncan, 2013), demonstrating that there was no lack of interest in girls playing. The arguments for girls playing cricket were rehearsed from those arguments that also encouraged boys to play, encouraging loyalty to the 'mother country', suggesting that women were supposed to identify with the nation in similar ways as men did. The fact that girls were educated separately from boys enabled girls to play a range of sports. As Hargreaves (1994) notes, one compliment paid to a headmistress about her school cricket team was: 'Your girls play like gentleman, and behave like ladies' (cited in Hargreaves, 1994: 68). Adhering to codes of femininity was necessary, but as these games took place in private, girls had access to playing games such as cricket. Women also began playing at colleges where there is no evidence to suggest that men actively discouraged women from playing the game. Guttmann (1991) suggests that this was because women largely played the game whilst adhering to strict behavioural codes, and simultaneously emphasising femininity, and thus they posed no direct challenge to men's sport and men's superiority in cricket.

It was not until the 1880s that the women's game began to develop more extensively and the first women's cricket club, The White Heather Club, emerged in 1887. Although comprised of a mix of single and married women, all were of independent means. In the club, three of the eight founding members were titled Lady, indicating that a particular class of women was involved in the game. The club quickly expanded from 8 players in 1887 to 50 by 1891 (Joy, 1950). One member of the club was Lucy Risdale, who was the elder daughter of Colonel Risdale; she later married conservative Prime Minister Stanley Baldwin. Two other clubs that emerged after this were the Dragonflies and the Clifton Ladies Club. Women were thought to be bowling both underarm and overarm at this time and there was great variation in standards of play. The emergence of new clubs indicates that girls and women were starting to play the game, although this was largely restricted to educational institutions and a few elite clubs, and McCrone (1988) points out that cricket was a much less popular sport for women than hockey.

In the 1890s a different club emerged; the Original English Lady Cricketers (OELC) was formed by the English Cricket and Athletic Association to profit from a women's touring team. The women who played were predominantly from the lower middle classes and they used the opportunity to earn money from the game. Joy (1950) suggests that the matches, which were exhibition matches, were stage-managed. The emergence of the team suggests that there was a view that the women's game could be commercialised, a view that seemed quite advanced for its time. The OELC was managed by men and the women were also professionally coached by men. Teams were sponsored and dressed by Lillywhites, each player was given a bat and uniform and exhibition matches were played on county pitches. Sponsorship of the teams suggests that women playing sport could attract commercial interest. The women who played were protected in several ways; they had pseudonyms and a matron accompanied the women on tour. These measures were taken to ensure that the women's respectability was maintained. At the opening match played on the Police Athletic Ground in Liverpool on Easter Monday in 1890, there were 15,000 spectators and one match report noted that people 'came to scoff and remained to praise' (Heyhoe Flint and Rheinberg, 1976: 26). Some spectators were there out of novelty interest in women playing cricket. Most of the reports suggest that the women involved were unmarried and young, indicating that the game was considered inappropriate for married women with family commitments. Reports suggest that women bowled overarm; therefore a certain standard of play was evident. However, the team disbanded within two years amid rumours that the managers absconded with the profits (Heyhoe Flint and Rheinberg, 1976).

This form of cricket was not viewed positively by lady cricketers and one of the reasons for this is that playing for money was not viewed as appropriate. This mirrors similar debates and tensions about professionals and amateurs in men's cricket and also reflects broader class relations about playing for profit. The cricket media largely ignored the OELC but the wider press did comment positively on the women's involvement; nevertheless, with this came a reassurance that 'ladies could never expect to challenge men on anything like equal terms' (McCrone, 1988: 146). Later establishment texts on women's cricket, such as Joy's (1950) history of the women's game, indicate the scant regard that lady cricketers had for the OELC. One of the reasons for this may have been the early views of professionalisation in the women's game which were frowned upon and were against the code of the Women's Cricket Association (WCA). After the OELC disbanded, the women's game continued through ladies' clubs such as White Heather. Social Class was a distinct factor in women's involvement in the early forms of the game and there were varying views on what type of cricket was considered appropriate for women. Women from a particular class were able to play cricket, away from public scrutiny. However these women were careful to ensure they played with propriety and, furthermore, they did not challenge the dominance of the men's game.

When the OELC disbanded in 1892, the men's game had had an organising body for over 100 years. During this time, various forms of women's cricket were played, but there was no unified organised body developing or lobbying for the game; rather the game was organised by individuals and was played more sporadically, perhaps indicating a type of harmonious inequality, a term used by Van Stolk and Wouters (1987) to explain how the outsider group is more likely to identify with the established group than vice versa. A key characteristic of established and outsider relations is that the established view remains embedded in the personality of the outsiders. Women cricketers accepted the view that men's cricket reflected a type of English masculinity and did not seek to challenge this; thus although women played, they did not challenge the core belief that cricket was a male sport and that men were superior at the game. This position allowed women to play cricket as they did not threaten the established group that allowed women to play, and nor did they show interest in organising, developing or supporting the game.

The emergence and maintenance of male-only institutions enabled men to monopolise key resources, finances, pitches, the decisions made about laws and the image of cricket as being a male sport. Although this may not have been a conscious effort to exclude women, but was rather more indicative of social relations between the sexes at the time in which men and women had different experiences in public life and different leisure activities, and women were still largely confined to the domestic sphere. Power relations between men and women cricketers at this stage were tilted in favour of the established group; there is still little evidence of women taking up the game seriously at this time, and wider debates about women and sport continued to focus on medical discourses that circulated about women's bodies being unsuitable for certain types of sports and exercise. The medical discourses were also widely accepted by men and women who viewed sports for women as improper.

The discussions about women's cricket in mainstream cricket literature are few and far between; yet in 1893, Richard Daft, a cricket player who wrote *Kings of Cricket*, suggested that if women were to play, they would need an adapted form of the game, for example, a lighter bat and a shorter pitch. These comments reflected a view that largely accepted women as being physically weaker and that, therefore, if they were going to play, they would need an adapted form of the game, which is what happened in most sports to allow women's involvement. These views were largely drawn from medical advice that placed women's involvement in sport as problematic and firmly considered male and female bodies to have differing physical capabilities, and from male (and female) doctors who debated the role of exercise and sport for women (Hargreaves, 1994). In fact Daft's suggestion was never implemented or taken seriously and given that there was no organisational governance of the women's game and that few women played, the need for such adaptations was not felt.

By the end of the 19th century, the perception of cricket as being a male sport was firmly embedded in the habitus of men and women. Cricket reflected a type of English masculinity (Malcolm, 2013) that was accepted by men and women. In the personalities of men and women, social activities between the sexes were predominately separate, and whilst there is evidence that women supported the men's game, their involvement in playing was negotiated in a way that did not challenge the position of the established group. Women's cricket was also divided by class; the experiences of ladies and the development of ladies' clubs were in vast contrast to the OELC, a team made up of professionals playing for money. The men's game had developed the game extensively; cricket had undergone a diffusion process and was now played across the colonies (mainly by men) and women's involvement was still marginal. It was not until after World War I (WWI) that a formal governing body for women's cricket emerged and it is to this formation that I now turn.

The formation of the England Women's Cricket Association

During and after WWI, there was a shift in power relations between the sexes, predominantly the result of more women working during the war, which meant that they entered the labour market. This changed the sexual division of labour; after the war although many women went back into the home, some continued to work and others stayed involved in the leisure activities that they had joined during the war. This, in addition to the suffragette movement, acknowledged women's ability to make political decisions, something previously considered unworthy of women. These political changes were significant as they illustrated a shift in power relations in which men had less power to control key areas such as politics (Brinkgreve, 2004). These changes were therefore indicative of a process of functional democratisation and although power relations remained unequal, there was a trend towards equalisation, which meant that women began to have greater access to political and social life. These changes also required changes at the level of psychogenesis in which men and women became more interdependent and identified with one another to a greater extent. These processes were part of larger social changes and they accompanied changes and standards of emotional control in men and women, as external restraint became more internalised because the views of women had to be taken into greater consideration. As some women had the vote, men could no longer ignore the needs and wishes of women voters; girls and women (of a certain class) had access to education and, through education, were able to play a range of sports (McCrone, 1988). There continued to be differences in relation to social class, as upper- and middle-class women had more opportunities to be involved in games than working-class girls.

These processes were not without tension, as the response to the suffragette movement was fought through public demonstrations and not all men and women were supportive of the votes-for–women movement. Furthermore there was resistance towards the suffragettes, although the response was not overly violent as it was becoming increasingly unacceptable for the state to use violence against women in this regard and negotiation was considered a more appropriate way to consider disputes.

There were distinct class relations in women's sport at this time and social expectations of women's behaviour and differing codes of femininity in different social classes were evident. Upper-class women in particular had a vested interest in adhering to established views about civilised women as adherence to such views ensured marriage, which was a way of securing a particular lifestyle. Harmonious inequality thus demonstrates a figurational ideal in which the outsider group identifies with the established group as it benefits from this in some way, that is, material or financial protection. Ideas about women and civilised behaviour were reinforced by institutions such as the medical profession and the church, which were influential in defining women's roles as mothers. Women were considered the gentler sex and were also viewed as a civilising influence on others. This view of women militated against the involvement of women in certain activities and in diverse forms of physical activities, especially in the middle and upper classes in which ladylike behaviour was a behavioural ideal largely accepted by men and women (Hargreaves, 1994). There is evidence to suggest that women watched men's sport and supported men's cricket, suggesting that they also were interested in watching sport and supporting the nation. When women played sport, they did so according to conventions that would not challenge their social relationships and interdependencies with men, often doing so in separate spaces and organisations away from public scrutiny.

In 1926 the England Women's Cricket Association (EWCA) was formed; this coincided with the development of other women's sports governing bodies, such as the All England Netball Association and the All England Women's Lacrosse Association, which was formed in 1912. Although the All England Women's Hockey Association (AEWHA) was formed in 1896, this is significant because of the overlap between the women who played cricket and hockey. Discussions about the formation of the EWCA had been going on for some time between women players, and during a cricket gathering at Colwall near Malvern, a group of hockey players who also played cricket discussed whether an association was appropriate (Joy, 1950). The discussions about the appropriateness of an organisation highlight women's concerns about how their involvement might be viewed by others. The women were conscious of the association of cricket with masculinity and the nation and of cricket as a national sport. They were aware that the grounds and key facilities belonged to male cricketers and that any organisation emerging or forming would need to be sensitive to these issues (Heyhoe Flint and Rheinberg, 1976). From the outset an established outsider figuration was influencing the behaviour of the outsider group as embedded in the personalities of the outsiders was the view that cricket was a male sport; from these initial discussions, it can be seen that there was a need for the outsider group to consider the views of the established group in a way that would not be reciprocated (for example, the MCC were not concerned about the views of women's cricketers or whom they might offend).

On 4 October 1926 a committee was formed at a meeting in London; Mrs Patrick Heron-Maxwell was the first chairman of the organisation. Eleven members were part of the committee of which nine were unmarried, suggesting that unmarried women may have had more freedom for leisure activities than married women. Links between cricket and hockey were evident as the chairman had also been president of the AEWHA and she had worked in the Land Army during the war. Another committee member, Miss Cox, had captained the England women's hockey team in 1911. The members of the EWCA committee were upper-class women of independent means and their concern from the beginning was to 'enable any women or girl wishing to play cricket to do so and to play the game with strict order and decorum' (Heyhoe Flint and Rheinberg, 1976: 31). In order to ensure that this could be monitored in the 1926 report, it was suggested that the committee needed to have 'knowledge of the suitability of those wishing to become members' (WCA, 1926: 2). The need to ensure propriety and control membership was in part to ensure that the organisation did not offend the established male group and to ensure that women cricketers adhered to behavioural expectations of upper-/middle-class women.

In the first year the membership of the EWCA reached 300 and ten clubs were formed. Cricket week, an annual gathering, was organised in 1927 with 40 players attending. The number of members within the first year reflects how many women were playing prior to the formation of the EWCA. It is unlikely that the organisation rapidly developed the game but rather the organisation offered unified governance for the women's game that clubs decided to join. A common concern found in the minutes and yearbooks continued to be about decorum and the dress and behaviour of women cricketers. In order to control the image of the women's game, in 1928 the EWCA outlined regulations of dress that stipulated;:

> WCA teams must play in cream or white. Hats or knickers must be white. Dresses and tunics must not be shorter than touching the ground when kneeling. Sleeveless dresses and transparent stockings are not permitted (WCA, 1928: 1).

Written rules stipulating dress demonstrate an ongoing concern about ensuring that women cricketers were viewed in the best possible way and did not challenge dominant ideas about femininity and propriety. For this reason the EWCA did not agree to a public match in 1929; prior to this, matches had taken place on private grounds. The decision to hold a public match was not taken lightly, and many members were against the idea and thought public matches were inappropriate. One of the reasons for this was also the press commentary at the time and the fact that bad press was difficult to 'live down' (Joy, 1950: 36). The EWCA seemed to have been concerned about press reports, and in 1929, after the agreement of a public match, Marjorie Pollard volunteered to produce an EWCA magazine as well as write commentary for the *Morning Post* and *London Evening News*. The organisation members were more than aware of the type of press commentary on the women's game and were conscious that they did not want negative publicity that might influence the established group's perception of the women's game.

Concern over dress and press continued in the 1930s, and one such discussion in 1930 amongst the committee members considered banning the press at matches. Other rules were published in WCA magazines, such as a reminder for women and girls to 'keep their leg guards clean' (1930: 11). Concern with women's dress was not unusual at the time; as Skillen (2012) argues, this reflects wider social issues about the female body, especially during the interwar years. Female dress often courted comments from others, as this signals broader discussions about women's freedom and sexuality. Sports dress in particular was problematic as a balance was needed between fashion, femininity, respectability, and practicality. Women's involvement in sport in the interwar years was contested and courted controversy and this is extensively reflected in the WCA reports, yearbooks and magazines.

From the outset there was opposition to the formation and development of the WCA and this was often very open. For example, in the first edition of the WCA's monthly magazine, one gentleman declared,

> Cricket for females is a preposterous idea, I felt sorrow and dismay at the idea that another field of male activities was to be usurped by the fairer sex, cricket is degraded . . . let us have this one sport to ourselves (WCA, 1930: 8).

Such open disagreement to the organisation demonstrates that expressing such opinion was not considered inappropriate, and the fact that the EWCA chose to print this in its own magazine demonstrates that it fully understood the opposition to women playing cricket and somehow wanted to combat this by demonstrating this awareness. The EWCA did not offer any resistance or comment to the reader, thus suggesting that in printing this letter it also wanted to make sure that the EWCA members understood their potential to offend male cricketers and to encourage members to adhere to behaviour codes which did not offend and did not overtly challenge the established group.

In order to combat any potential to offend or at least to ensure that hostility was reduced, women tried to ensure that the women's game remained separate from the men's game and were keen to ensure that the women's game was in no way positioned as a sport that might threaten the men's game. As Pollard states, 'We recognised our limitations, no one tried to bowl too fast, cricket of our own, we did not want to play cricket like men, we wanted to play women's cricket' (1933: 30). Women cricketers largely accepted, or at least did not challenge, the differences in the ideology of women's weakness or the view that they would not play cricket as well as men. As the established group monopolised all the key resources in the game, more broadly the women did not have the capacity to 'challenge' the established group. This acceptance of the group's disgrace and lack of resistance was the consequence of being an outsider group, but critically it did enable women to play the game separately from the men's game and women were able to quietly develop the women's game away from public scrutiny and to promote the game as being separate from men's cricket. This enabled the game to develop in a specific way as an organisation run by women for women, keen not to challenge the established group. Therefore in the early forms of the game and the formation of the EWCA, a form of harmonious inequality existed, and as women cricketers were so dependent on men for resources (i.e. pitches), this relationship continued with little resistance from either the established or the outsider group. The emergence of cricket for women in Australia developed slightly differently and it is to the emergence and development of the women's game in Australia that I now turn.

Australian Cricket and gender relations and Australia

The development of men's cricket in Australia is linked to the colonial relationship between Australia and England. Cricket was diffused and played in Australia from 1803 and the game was played in an 'English' way. Club names mimicked English clubs, and at the cricket grounds, English trees were planted in an attempt to recreate English cricket landscapes and English village cricket (Cashman, 1998). Cricket in Australia came to play a role in debates about colonialism and the relationship between England and Australia politically. Australian cricket was played by more individuals from different social classes than early forms of English cricket but those who controlled and organised the game came largely from the dominant classes (Cashman, 1998). From the outset cricket was viewed as a male sport, and when played it reflected masculinity, either form of English or Australian masculinity which was linked to ideas of gender, nation and national identity. However at this time there is no doubt that the ideological status of cricket was to promote a manly game (Cashman, 1998). Whilst there were tensions in the game around class and race, women's cricket was not played regularly and was not a key part of the development of the game.

Women's early role in Australian cricket was one of spectatorship, with little evidence that they played the game extensively. In the 19th century, ladies' stands were built at key stadiums, indicating that a number of women did watch matches and thus must have supported the men's game, albeit in separate social spaces than men, again highlighting how men and women would socialise separately (Cashman and Weaver, 1991). A match report in 1832 mentioned how there were many respectable ladies in attendance and that the ladies' presence at matches was encouraged; one might relate this to the idea that women's presence might civilise the crowd. Men's cricket tours were popular between 1861 and 1862, and when Australia and England played against one another, large crowds were drawn to matches. These matches and their results began to represent a decline in imperial rule as debates raged cricket increasingly became a form of expression for Australian nationalism. Australians wanted to beat the motherland at their own game and saw defeating England as representing a decline in imperial rule and a belief that the English could be beaten (Mandle, 1973). This enabled cricket to be used as a form of national identity; beating the motherland at cricket represented beating the coloniser and could strengthen the otherwise-quite-fragmented notions of national identity, based on the complexities of the Australian nation state and its formation. As Australian women also watched matches, women were likely to support the game and this suggests that women also saw the game as reflecting national identity and thus raises interesting questions about the role of gender in the formation of national identities.

Australian men's cricket did not have a governing body until 1905 when the Australian Board of Control for International Cricket (ABCIC) was formed. This organisation was created solely to develop, organise and promote men's cricket, govern the game and develop international tours.

The emergence of women's cricket in Australia

The first women's cricket match is believed to be an unconfirmed match in 1815, with other matches in New South Wales (NSW) in 1855, but reports are sporadic and there is little evidence that women played the game extensively. The first recorded women's match was in Bendigo, Victoria, in 1874 and this is likely to coincide with the England men's tour to Australia that year (Heyhoe Flint and Rheinberg, 1976). This match received negative press coverage and focused on ladies' fashion rather than the style of play. It was presented as a one-off match and even those playing did not intend for the women's cricket matches to be repeated (Duncan, 2013). Thus cricket around this time for women seems not to have been played very frequently and there is little mention of women's involvement other than to spectate at men's matches.

The next-recorded match was in 1886 and was held on 8 March, between two teams, the Siroccos and the Fernleas. All the women who played in this match were unmarried, suggesting that marriage and cricket were not entirely compatible for women and that unmarried women may have had more opportunity to be involved (Cashman and Weaver, 1991). The match was a charity match specifically marketed for raising money for a charity event, and was attended by 1,000 spectators. A later match in April 1886 played at the Sydney Cricket Ground (SCG) had 3,500 spectators. The fact that these were charity matches enabled women to play without too much scrutiny as, by focusing on good causes and not serious cricket, the women ensured that they were not challenging the position of the men's game and nor were they challenging the behavioural codes of femininity. Despite this, these games seemed to be the catalyst for future developments as matches between city and country sides were played; as more matches were played, the press commentary became more derogatory, and the game was largely considered a joke (Cashman and Weaver, 1991).

In contrast to the English game that at a similar time was rather shielded in the public schools and universities, the public matches in Australia courted more media attention and with it more criticism. The game was played in more areas than others, including in Victoria and NSW; in 1891 a match was again played at the SCG. Media reports suggested that the women's game was not of a worthy standard of play, suggesting that 'from what we have seen of the bowling . . . we feel sure that it will never be of any value until the distance between the wickets is reduced to 20 yards'. The comparison between men's and women's cricket was made at this public match, which resulted in the idea of reducing the field of play. This was to enable women to play, but it also enabled comparisons to be made between men and women that would ensure women's cricket and its players were viewed as weaker, a common discourse of the time. This view draws on established perceptions about the outsider group, derived from notions of group disgrace in which the female body is positioned as inferior to the male sporting body and therefore for women to play special considerations are needed.

It was not until 1902 that girls' cricket was played in Australian schools and this can be explained by significant broader social processes occurring at this time. In particular, women were admitted to universities in 1881 and property and divorce rights were granted in the 1890s; arguably these two issues are significant broader social processes that suggest an equalising trend in gender relations at this time, and a stage of emancipation and resistance (Van Stolk and Wouters, 1987). This is further evidenced by Australian women being granted the right to vote in 1902, which was much earlier than in England in 1918.

The role of women's suffrage in advancing women's sport in Australia seems to have been more overt than in England. For example, Vida Goldstein, a prominent voice in women's reforms, founded the Women's Federal Political Association in 1903 and was the first president of the Victoria Cricket League Association (VCLA), founded in 1905. This was the first organising body of women's cricket in Australia, although not a national governing body; this organisation was founded for organising women's cricket and advancing the women's game in the Victorian area. The link between politics and women's cricket demonstrates differences in the development of the game in different countries. Another significant difference between this organisation and organisations in England was that two of the vice presidents of VCLA were men and there were both male and female delegates at the first meeting, demonstrating that there was some support for the women's game from men who were actively involved in the organisation. This was different from the situation in England where men's involvement in the initial formation of the game was less apparent.

The increasing numbers of girls playing cricket in schools is notable at this time, albeit predominantly in private schools, which indicates that there was some class bias in the women's game (following a trend similar to the men's game). However, church organisations such as the Church of England Ladies Cricket Association which was formed in 1906 suggest that there was a growing acceptance of the women's game and these organisations might have been more accessible to a range of women. Interstate competitions were played from 1906 to 1910; this was before the emergence of a national governing body, again signalling a difference between the English and Australian contexts, as in England although cricket was played before the formation of the EWCA, formal competition was not part of this. In Australia the formation of the VCLA and other state bodies seemed to signal a beginning of competitive women's cricket. However, by 1916 the women's game was in decline; the reasons for this seem unclear but are related to the ridicule that women received from men. When women married, they were unlikely to continue playing and the team was short of money and facilities to play (Duncan, 2013). The VCLA was disbanded in 1916 and women's cricket was on the demise.

Around the time of the decline of women's cricket, another sport was being introduced: Vigoro was becoming popular among women in NSW. The sport was introduced in Australia in 1908 by Englishman John George Grant. The game, although not specifically designed for women, soon became known as a women's game. The game resembles cricket but it is played on a shorter wicket with a paddle-shaped bat. The sport was originally introduced for high-school boys but, due to cultural dominance of cricket, was not popular (Paolucci, 2010). Although some boys played until 12 years of age, the adult version of the game is for women only. Due to the cultural dominance of cricket as a male sport, it seems that women playing Vigoro were considered more acceptable. Vigoro continues to be a sport played predominantly by women and its emergence and acceptance as a women's sport may have suited the Victorian notions of modified sport for women.

Re-emergence of women's cricket and the Australian Women's Cricket Council

It was not until after WWI that there was a revival in women's cricket in Australia. In Victoria, matches were reinstated and the Victorian Women's Cricket Association was established in 1923. The change in the name from the Victorian Ladies Cricket Association to Victorian Women's Cricket Association indicated a more inclusive approach to the game and other factors such as the inclusion of factory teams seem to support this assertion (Cashman and Weaver, 1991). Interstate competitions resumed in the 1930s. The re-emergence of the women's game in the States led to the formation of the AWCC in 1931. The formation of the organisation that governed the game followed a meeting of women players who had gathered to discuss their concerns about the ridicule faced by women cricketers prior to WWI. The women were acutely aware of their potential to offend and were keen to consider ways to lessen this. The objectives of the AWCC were to

- Promote the development of women's cricket in Australia
- Make rules for the good government of women's cricket
- Arrange, control and regulate visits of teams to and from Australia
- Organise representative matches in Australia in which cricketers of more than one state are engaged
- Organise annual cricket matches between state women's cricket associations (Cashman and Weaver, 1991: 48).

At the start of the organisation not all areas were affiliated; Western and Southern Australia did not affiliate due to costs of sending teams to play, but in 1934, prior to the England tour, all areas affiliated to enable benefits to the areas involved. From the outset women's cricket in Australia was more competitive than in England, where winning and leagues were frowned upon, as amateur status was valued and playing for playing's sake was valued. In Australia interstate competitions were played; club cricket was competitive with a point system and at the end of each season a trophy was awarded. The formation of the AWCC was critical in enabling the first international game to be played when England toured Australia in 1934.

Harmonious inequality in Australian and English cricket

In a seminal paper on established and outsider figurations, Van Stolk and Wouters (1987) introduce the term harmonious inequality to refer to relations in which the established and outsider groups are dependent on one another. In these relations, outsiders are often rewarded by the established for specific behaviour which helps maintain unequal power relations; for instance, in gender relations women have often been rewarded for certain behaviour expectations through the economic security of marriage. Van Stolk and Wouters suggest that as an outsider group, women who abide by particular behavioural ideals as defined by the established group are rewarded with physical and material protection. Women who do not conform to these ideals can be made to feel their outsider status even more harshly. Outsider groups also internalise the view the established group may have of them, accepting the established view. Women internalise and sympathise with the established group as a strategy which can arguably enable them access to some resources without being too antagonistic.

In both the English and Australian contexts, the emergence of women's cricket was impacted on by the emergence of an established and outsider figuration in which men's cricket and male cricketers were firmly an established group. Cricket strongly reflected masculinity and nationality in both countries. A common issue in both countries is that for cricket to reflect masculinity and nationality women had to be discouraged or excluded from playing. However, in neither context were women physically banned from playing; instead ideologies about the game, alongside behavioural codes of femininity that were largely accepted by men and women, were strong enough to ensure that cricket was firmly viewed as first and foremost a male sport that reflected a form of national character associated with masculinity, colonialism and colonial power (or resistance).

In both Australia and England there were men who supported women playing cricket, albeit as a form of recreation, with the assumption that the women's game would never challenge the men's game. The balance of power between men's and women's cricket was tilted in favour of the men's game and power was firmly in the established group's favour. Men had codified the game, developed the first governing body and had diffused the game with varying success across the colonies; the sport was unquestionably masculine. Key resources such as money, facilities, the perception of masculinity and nationalism, as well as the formation of the International Cricket Council in 1909 ensured that men monopolised not only key physical resources but also ideological resources that positioned the game as a male game, one with national significance. Thus when women played the game, it was done so with no threat of physical challenge from the established group; the response of the established group was to ignore and at times to ridicule female players.

In England women were particularly keen to ensure that they did not challenge the men's game. They strongly accepted that men were better suited to the game and internalised the view that women were physically weaker than men, this is likely associated with the habitus and personalities of those involved who accepted the view that cricket was a male sport. This acceptance reflects Elias' wider view of gender relations in which he explains 'a kind of inequality that has been codified . . . in such a way it became not only custom but habit, part of the social habitus of individuals' (Elias, 1987: 287). Men's and women's cricket coexisted but men's domination of resources was not questioned by men or women, reflecting broader gender relations at the time of the EWCA's emergence. Men monopolised key resources in education and politics more broadly and women's views and rights were not widely considered important; whilst women had the vote, gender relations more broadly of this era were titled in favour of men.

It is important to also understand that women had a personal interest and also invested in codes of femininity, and that this was often related to social class. The women involved in the EWCA were from middle- and upper-class backgrounds and they gained access to cricket through less direct means; purposefully they did not seek to question men's power or make demands of the men's game, this was not unusual at the time and reflects broader issues in women's role in political and social life (Gleadle, 2009). The role of men in the EWCA was debated from the outset of the organisation's formation. In the minutes of the annual meeting in 1927, it was suggested that men should be 'invited to be honorary members of the organisation' (WCA, 1927: 4). This category of membership was proposed to thank men who supported the women's game. This is an interesting illustration of established and outsider relations as it is unlikely that the MCC would have considered a membership category to thank women who supported the men's game, made tea and provided other services to the game. The women's desire to thank men may be linked to the need to be accepted by the established group (and not to be seen as too political or challenging) and reflects the characteristics of established and outsider relations more broadly as the views and needs of the established group are firmly embedded in the personality and behaviour of outsiders (Van Stolk and Wouters, 1987).

In Australia women's cricket emerged in different contexts from those in England; there is little evidence of women's involvement in early forms of the game. The diffusion of cricket to Australia, at a time when cricket was strongly associated as a male sport that reflected forms of masculinity and national identity (both English and Australian) ensured that the women's game saw a formation of established and outsider figuration. In Australia, cricket reflected colonial tensions; men's cricket reflected forms of national identity and early organisations sought to support the development of men's cricket. The thought of women's cricket was far from the minds of male cricketers as power relations between the two groups were firmly in favour of men's cricket. Women's cricket emerged at a time in which women were gaining greater access to public life more broadly. Women's and men's cricket forms were seemingly more interdependent in Australia. Australian women had access to greater resources, for instance, key grounds such as the Melbourne Cricket Ground (MCG) and the SCG.

Early forms of women's cricket in the 1900s were played more publicly than in England at this time, and this courted response from the established group which was keen to ridicule women cricketers. This ridicule can be understood as a form of blame gossip used to ensure that the established group maintains its dominance. Thus greater interdependence may have enabled women cricketers greater access to resources; this had the effect of being both enabling and constraining as public matches courted a greater response from male cricketers keen to dissuade others from supporting the women's game or using blame gossip as a way of ensuring that women's cricket is positioned as a game on the margins of 'real cricket'.

The first international match and international tour

A peculiarity in cricket explored by Malcolm (2013) is that it is considered both an English and a British game. The game had different developments in Wales, Ireland and Scotland. In women's cricket, the first international match was played at Worcestershire's county ground between Scottish XI and English XI on 29 and 30 August 1932 (WCA Report, 1932). The England team was made up of several women from different teams, whereas the Scotland team was predominantly made up of those at St Leonards in St Andrews, as the game in Scotland was significantly less developed and geographically located predominantly in the St Andrews area. England won the match; this was expected given the more established team and the match report suggests that the quality of bowling on the Scottish side was generally poor. The WCA was keen to thank the authorities for allowing them 'use of ground' (1932: 13). The need to thank the authorities not once but twice in one document demonstrates the reliance of the women's game on the established group and the eagerness of the outsider group to be seen as grateful.

The first women's international tour was arranged between the AWCC and the EWCA in 1934. The first tour was considered to be significant by all involved; an article in the *Women's Weekly* on 24 November 1934 (Australia) reported:

> To the Australian players this tour means a great deal . . . To occupy the leading pages in the newspapers, to be photographed, and to know that their names are being broadcast through the commonwealth and England adds glamour to the scene. (Preddey, cited in Cashman and Weaver, 1991: 84)

The England team sailed in 1934 and according to Joy (1950) the team that sailed were not a representative side and this was partly due to 'financial and other reasons'. Playing for England was problematic for some women who could not afford the time and money to play; each English player had to pay £80 and purchase her own equipment – this was an extensive amount of money for the time; as Cashman and Weaver (1991) suggest, this amount was equivalent to 43 weeks of the average female salary. Day-to-day expenses were covered by the host country and the AWCC expected some money to be raised through gate money revenue. The tour rules were strict: a ban on husbands or friends travelling with players; a prohibition of drinking, gambling and smoking; and an insistence that players be in bed by 10:00 p.m. Players were not allowed to write articles on matches. The reasons for these strict codes were to ensure propriety during the tour; these behavioural codes were firmly embedded in the attitudes of women players and those organising the tour such that women behaved in specific ways that the established group would approve of. The tour was popular amongst spectators and the first match played at the Western Australian Cricket Association (WACA) received 3,500 spectators. This should be viewed in relation to recent events in the men's game at this time. The men had played a recent Ashes series and there had been controversy over bodyline bowling. In response to this, Betty Archdale, captain of the English side, was keen to stress that 'we are not here for any Ashes but merely to play cricket' (cited in Cashman and Weaver, 1991: 85). This may in part explain the desire on the part of women to not call their series 'the Ashes' and also stresses the policy of ensuring that the men's and women's games stay separate and different. Throughout the tour, the women were greeted by dignitaries and had numerous civic receptions; attendances throughout the tour remained high. As Cashman and Weaver (1991) note, the majority of the crowd comprised men, and this seems to be reflective of cricket audiences more broadly and also broader issues around women's and men's leisure time; men had more time to spend watching cricket whether it be men's or women's games. England won the series easily, but the tour was successful, considering the crowds and interest created. Not all press responses were positive and some were keen to stress the differences between the men's and women's games; for example, the *Courier Mail* (29 December 1934, cited in Cashman and Weaver, 1991: 93) stated:

> If the girls lacked the strength of men players, the spectators found compensation in their graceful bearing and willowy movements.

There were some comments about how male sports may well masculinise women; in particular the appearance of Betty Archdale was commented on by some as being boyish. Yet like Pollard in England, in Australia the *Women's Weekly* sports editor was Ruth Preddey and she wrote extensive match reports in the magazine. As mentioned previously, the bodyline series was often brought up and it was commented on how women were more 'civilised' in their approach to the game. Perhaps for some cricket fans who expected the game to be played in specific ways that are linked to issues of class and identity, the women were perceived to play a fair game. As Archdale notes, 'People were relieved to find that we could play cricket without trying to kill the other side' (cited in Cashman and Weaver, 1991: 94). The tour established international women's cricket, and a return tour was organised to England in 1937. The revenue from the 1934 tour also enabled the AWCC to partially fund the tour to England.

Concluding thoughts

This chapter started by looking at early forms of women's involvement in cricket and the subsequent re-emergence of cricket as a male preserve. The development of cricket as a male preserve constrained women's involvement in the game. The dual processes of parliamentarisation and sportisation involved primarily men. Cricket was firmly established as a sport that enhanced masculinity and reflected ideal views of Englishness, and women's involvement in the sport was restricted by social processes that focused on cricket and masculinity and on broader social processes that devalued women's involvement in the nation, politics and other fields of economic and social value. Male cricketers also monopolised key resources needed to play cricket, facilities, and ideological control over rules. This monopoly of resources is critical in considering unequal power balances between the two groups; as the established and outsider figuration emerges, power is tilted extensively in favour of males.

The response to women playing cricket was not however violent; instead the power relations between the two groups was unbalanced in a way that women did not challenge the view that men's cricket was the established sport. As an outsider group when women did create their own governing body, they did so knowing that there might be resistance to women's involvement in cricket. The male and female cricketers firmly accepted that men's cricket was the national game although the role of men in the AWCC and the EWCA was viewed differently, and in the AWCC, closer interdependency with men may have enabled access to better resources; such interdependency also led to more ridicule of female cricketers than in England where there was greater separation between men and women cricketers.

When the EWCA emerged in England, the women's game coexisted alongside, but separate from the men's game, and in a typical established and outsider figuration, female cricketers demonstrated more concern with the views, attitudes and needs of the male established group than vice versa. The diffusion of cricket in Australia as a male sport at a specific time when cricket reflected particular notions of English masculinity ensured that a similar established and outsider figuration emerged in which the male established group developed an organisation that focused on the men's game. Cricket in both countries then reflected a form of Englishness and then an Australian national identity that is related to tensions about colonial power as well as the development of a strong relationship among cricket, the nation and masculinity (i.e. ideas about being an Australian or English male).

Cricket was firmly established as a male sport, and women were prevented from playing cricket through strategies such as ridiculing their participation or through stressing biology or medical discourses that position women as outsiders. However women were not considered as threatening to the male establishment and so the response of the established group was not one of physical resistance. Power relations were firmly in favour of the established group, with neither the established nor the outsider group challenging this position. When the AWCC was formed in 1931, women's cricket was emerging in several areas, but similar to the English context, cricket was firmly accepted as a male sport and the AWCC did not challenge this perception. There are some differences in the development of cricket for women in Australia and England; in Australian women's cricket, the women were more interdependent upon the men's game, which offered opportunity, in relation to better facilities, but also constrained the development through greater opportunity to ridicule female cricketers; thus the response, for example, in the media was to draw more on blame gossip to ridicule the women's game and the women who played.

In both England and Australia, broader social processes that suggest long-term trends towards equalisation are of significance in understanding the development of women's access to cricket. For example, both governing bodies were formed after women had gained suffrage, a demonstration of a wider social process towards accepting women's increased involvement in political and social life. Women's increased access to education through the public schools and universities is also significant and was particularly relevant to the development of cricket for girls and women in England. The development of the governing bodies in both contexts was critical for the organisational development of the game, giving a central organising body to support and develop in each context. The emergence of the EWCA and the AWCC allowed for the development of international women's cricket. By the end of the 1930s, women's cricket was an international game with two international tours. This may well reflect a broader issue in relation to the popularity of cricket in the 1930s in England and Australia. In the following chapter I consider the diffusion, emergence and development of cricket in several cricketing nations, drawing on theoretical ideas of civilising processes and the theory of established and outsider relations to support this analysis.

3
Civilising Processes, Gender Relations and the Global Women's Game

As discussed in the introduction to the book, women's cricket is growing and continues to develop as part of the International Cricket Council (ICC) and in different nations, at different paces. However, this growth is not universal. Some countries are developing at a much faster pace than others, and some nations that play the women's game have a more established history than others. At times this pattern of development runs parallel to the development of men's cricket, but this is not the case in all contexts and the diffusion of men's cricket and the subsequent adoption, resistance or acceptance of women in the game varies across the globe. This no doubt is reflective of broader gender relations and power struggles between men and women in different nation states, in which women's involvement in sport is such a small, but significant, part. In Chapter 2, the focus was on the development and emergence of cricket in England and Australia, as these were the first countries involved in playing the women's game. These were the first international matches that were played between these two nations, signalling the emergence of international women's cricket from 1934 onwards. In this chapter, the focus is on understanding the emergence and development of women's cricket in a number of other nation states, considering the emergence and development of women's cricket alongside the development of men's cricket and the creation of distinct established and outsider relations.

The emergence and development of cricket in different nation states is discussed throughout this chapter. In doing so, it is not my intention to provide a detailed historical sequential outline of cricket in each country but rather to offer a processual understanding of the emergence of women's cricket considering broader social processes that enabled and constrained the women's game in the following countries: Holland, Ireland, Pakistan, India, South Africa, New Zealand, Sri Lanka and the West Indies. These countries have been selected as they are the key nations currently competing in international cricket, and whilst Bangladesh and Zimbabwe are in the ICC full membership category, neither has a women's team that competes regularly in the global game. Ireland and Holland are discussed as countries which have had an early influence or part in the International Women's Cricket Council (IWCC) despite the relative low levels of men's cricket in their respective countries.

For each country discussed, I explore how cricket has diffused as a male sport, drawing on broader social processes and struggles in the game more broadly. I then consider how cricket came to reflect types of masculinity and nationality in each context. The emergence of women's cricket and the level of interdependency between men's and women's cricket in each country need to be considered alongside the formation of a governing body for the women's game. Finally in each country the nature of mutual power balances between men's and women's cricket and how gender relations and civilising processes (through functional democratisation) have impacted, and continue to impact on opportunities for women to play cricket.

Cricket and gender relations in India

Men's cricket has been played in India from 1721 and the first club was founded in 1792 in Calcutta. As cricket was exclusively played by the British in India, the first club was for Europeans only (Duncan, 2013). The first club for Indian players was founded much later in Bombay in 1848. The timing of this is significant as it is after the codification and reinvention of the game as a civilised sport (Majumdar, 2003). At this time cricket was generally viewed by the British as a sport that could civilise the population by introducing British standards and behaviour to an indigenous population that was considered unruly (Mustafa, 2013). With the establishment of colleges for the elite Indian communities, cricket played a significant role in training boys in English values. At these schools, headmasters and teachers, who were usually European, ensured that the elite group was able to maintain control over the indigenous population. Thus cricket was adopted in these schools as part of an imperial system and was viewed as a civilising and educating device.

Later, cricket was played to a greater extent by the Parsi community. The Parsis are a wealthy group who were closely linked to the British and heavily involved in trade activities. The first tournament introduced was the Bombay Pentangular Tournament, founded with the European, Hindu, Muslim and Parsi teams (all male). Alongside the Parsis, Indian princes also developed an interest in the game and their involvement followed a pattern similar to the amateur and professional divide in England. Princes would not bowl and field and this meant an opening for non-elite players to play as they would be paid to bowl and field at princes. Indian princes would also finance the team and players and in doing so would pay coaches from England and Australia to train players. This created competitive teams and was influential in developing an individual player's talent. In all these examples cricket was firmly established as a male sport from the outset, and all forms of cricket at that time excluded women.

The formation of the Board of Control for Cricket in India (BCCI) occurred in 1927; it was a male-only organisation focusing on developing Indian cricket, after its formation India played its first test match against England in 1932. Gradually, cricket in India became less controlled by the British, and through this process, Indians, particularly those in the mercantile or elite groups, were able to play the game away from the British. These teams were financed by emerging elite groups; as such cricket gradually began to reflect a type of Indian nationalism, separate from the British elite.

Independence from Britain in 1947 signalled a key time in the history of cricket in India. During this process of independence cricket came to reflect a type of nationalism that was encouraged by the new nation state. Cricket was also supported by state-owned companies such as the Indian Railways and privately owned companies such as the Tatas, which meant that the game was financed and supported by elite groups that had the money to promote the game. At this time cricket continued to be popular in urban areas (and amongst elite groups). Thus the advancement of media revolutionised the game from being a popular sport in certain areas to a national sport. Cricket received extensive media coverage because it was financed by the elite and by businesses that popularised the sport through media forums.

These media forums were able to ensure that the whole population understood the game through radio chat shows and discussions about the game. In these media accounts, the laws of the game and intricacies of the rules were discussed, alongside the personalities of those who played the game, thus promoting certain players and aspects of the game that came to reflect Indian nationalism. Through the media focus, male players became national heroes, and this ensured that cricket, as a sport, came to dominate.

Cricket developed into a national game, extensively discussed in media forums and in televised and radio shows. The male stars were also closely linked to the endorsement of products and stars reflected a form of imagined national identity in which India was presented as united through cricket, but also as part of a larger national identity that drew on colonial power relations and a desire to beat the old colonisers at their game. Thus cricket was diffused as a colonial sport but was reinvented as a national sport which was supported by the majority of Indians from different social classes and religious backgrounds and crucially was also supported by women who accepted Indian cricket stars as reflecting a form of national identity. Through diffusion, colonialism and post-colonialism, cricket was firmly established as a male sport and there is little evidence of women's involvement in the early accounts of the game. It seems that women were involved in spectating (Naha, 2012) and women have also supported the men's game and the national team.

The emergence of women's cricket in India

Early records of women playing are few and far between. Like men's cricket, cricket for girls was diffused by white women who set up charitable schools for girls. The game is thought to have been introduced by an Australian teacher at the Baker Memorial School in Kerala in 1913, where it was made compulsory for all girls (Heyhoe Flint and Rheinberg, 1976). The school was a mission school and one of the first girls' schools in India. Reflecting broader social issues, education for girls was not compulsory or necessarily valued for indigenous girls. It is not clear at this stage what role cricket played in the mission school or what ideological associations existed between cricket and the role of cricket in 'civilising' indigenous girls. There might have been an impetus to get girls to play sport, or there might have been a view that cricket could help civilise girls in the same way it was viewed as being a civilising sport for boys. These issues have not been considered in the literature about the diffusion of sport, which often ignores women's and girls' sport.

It was not until after independence that the women's game appears to have developed momentum, especially in Delhi where tournaments were held in the 1950s. This is significant as women began to have more freedom and more rights in urban contexts. Patchy reports of the women games continue in Delhi and Bombay, but until the formation of the Women's Cricket Association of India (WCAI) in 1973, the game lacked governance and reports of women and girls playing are few and far between.

The first interstate national matches were held in Pune in 1973, suggesting that there must have been a number of women playing prior to the formation of the WCAI. The WCAI was quick to join the IWCC in 1973 and invited a team to tour in 1975. The secretary of the WCAI was a male, which suggests there was support by some men, and which may have been needed in the wider context of gender relations at the time. The first tour was scheduled to coincide with the International Year of the Woman (Butcher, 1996). The Australian tour manager, Butcher recalls that at the start of the tour, not all members of the WCAI were supportive of the idea of a tour and 'many believed a team with English heritage would not be accepted by the Indian team' (1996: 1). This suggested some race-relations tensions in the women's game although little else is commented on in this regard. The Australian Women's Cricket Council (AWCC) agreed to the tour but it was not part of the formal IWCC schedule but rather a friendly tour, reflecting the fact that the Indian team were new to international competition. The AWCC requested volunteers who were willing to pay for their own travel costs and decided that a team of under-25 (U25) players would be most appropriate. Butcher who was the manager of the Australian team was also a member of the IWCC; therefore she was acutely aware of the need for the women's game to develop more substantially as the IWCC was struggling to develop an international governing body (see Chapter 4) and at this time had stagnated in its development. The tour was drawn, demonstrating that the Indian team were able to play cricket at an international level, despite much less experience. Media interest in the tour was extensive, with reports suggesting there were crowds of 20,000–40,000 spectators and matches were covered on radio and news.

Women's cricket in India has continued to grow and develop despite the general view that cricket is a sport for men; it has coexisted alongside the men's game but remained relatively separate. Cricket remains one of the few sports in which women can gain financial independence from men. The Indian media do support the women's game, yet this is far less extensive than the support extended to the men's game. However, there is a complex picture that emerges in support for the game, for example, many schools do not allow girls to play, suggesting there is some objection to women playing the sport (Thadani et al., 2012). Women cricketers often come from lower-middle-class backgrounds and see the sport as a way of supporting themselves with few opportunities for independent financial support (Gupta, 2013).

Men's cricket is the popular national sport; it symbolises national success and this is something that Indian women's cricketers do not represent. The focus on men's cricket and national identity remains largely unchallenged:

> The disproportionate national importance of men's cricket creates gendered images, and the symbolic marginalisation of women validates and reinforces these images (Gupta, 2013: 100)

Gupta (2013) suggests that this is part of a wider issue about women and gender relations more broadly. Looking at gender relations and the mutual power balance between men and women may be of importance here. In India violence against women is not always punished by the state, and marital rape is not a crime (Raj and McDougal, 2014). This, alongside the suggestion that only 1% of victims report rape as a crime, and national and local approaches to sexual violence indicate that gender relations in the country are varying which has received recent global media attention. State monopoly of deterrent punishment for violence against women is critical in the process of functional democratisation and in reducing power relations between men and women, which in turn allows women greater opportunity for work, education and financial stability and also opportunities to be involved in sport, state monopoly of violence is critical in equalising gender relations (Dunning, 1999). Thus, power balances between men and women in this context continue to largely favour males, and in this environment, the opportunity for women to access facilities and challenge dominant power relations is more difficult.

Cricket in India remains a sport that invokes nationalism but this nationalism is gendered: it is men's cricket which enhances people's view of the 'nation', as Majumdar (cited in Steen, 2010: 95) suggests:

> The fortunes of the Indian cricket team encapsulate the story of postcolonial India in microcosm; a tapestry permanently being woven around the performance of eleven men who carry on their shoulders the demands of a billion.

This statement clearly refers to the men's team's success; it is eleven 'men' who carry this expectation, although the 'demands of the billion' presumably also refers to women who also support the cricket team and also accept this men's team as a symbol of national identity. Women's success in cricket does not evoke such strong feelings of nationalism and some recent issues relating to the number of matches women play remain problematic. Thus the established game remains the men's game.

Recent changes in the women's game have been that the WCAI merged with the BCCI in 2006. This was part of the ICC mandate requesting all national governing bodies to represent men's and women's cricket. Since then developments in the game have been mixed, with increased interdependency at an organisational level, but one aspect of the game that has reduced is international competitions, especially test match cricket, and matches have generally been played in ICC tournaments with other tours occurring less frequently. The merger increases the interdependency between groups and becomes a power resource for the women's game as women's cricket cannot be ignored by those who organise and run the game. Yet such organisational shifts do not directly result in attitudinal changes and the game continues to be sex segregated; of interest in the Indian context is that the merger happened because of the ICC mandate which forced it to happen which means that the social habituses of those involved may not have wanted the women's game to be part of the BCCI and suggests that gender relations and mutual power balances between the men's and women's game are extensive. Inequities still exist; for example, domestic tournaments have become less frequent than before the merger. Cricket academies continue to remain male only, and the opportunity to make money from cricket remains firmly in the hands of the established group that developed and marketed the professional and commercial elements of the game. For example, the Indian Premier League (IPL), which is a male-only league that attracts the best international players who play on the same team. As men's cricket in India has developed, the BCCI has become the most prosperous national board (Steen, 2010), yet women's cricket is not as forthcoming and certainly not as financially viable or beneficial to players; power (im)balances between men's and women's cricket remain and are likely to continue to do so given the established nature of men's cricket and the strong relationship between the nation, masculinity, national identity and men's cricket, all factors which I argue impact on the development of women's cricket.

Cricket and gender relations in Pakistan

On 14 August 1947 Pakistan was formed as an independent country (it had formerly been part of India). Early elements of the development of cricket in Pakistan and its diffusion are rooted in Indian cricket. Pakistan is a relatively new nation state that has significant army control over part of its administrative and political state and there have been ongoing issues in relation to the stability of the state (Jan, 2010). As a nation state, Pakistan is often viewed by others as struggling to gain control over levels of violence and political stability, as state monopoly of violence is critical in civilising processes, the stability of Pakistan as a nation state continues to be problematic. As a country, particularly post-9/11, it is often viewed by others as a corrupt, linked to terrorism, violent and 'uncivilised' country, with backward views of gender democracy and religion. These views are often represented through discussions of Pakistani cricket (Malcolm, 2013) in which the other is often used as a form of blame gossip.

Cricket is the national sport of Pakistan and it is closely tied to social and political life (Bandyopadhyay, 2007). The Board of Control for Cricket in Pakistan (BCCP) was formed in 1949, and shortly after, in 1952, Pakistan was admitted to the ICC. Cricket has an established history and the BCCP was formed, as most governing bodies were, to support men's cricket. Perhaps reflecting wider political issues, the BCCP has often been viewed as a corrupt and an unstable organisation in its governance of the game. Despite this, cricket is the national sport and is popular not only within the country itself but also among those in the Pakistani diaspora who support their national side and see cricket as reflecting a form of national identity that is important to Pakistani communities (Valiotis, 2009). This support is seen in the Pakistani diaspora in Britain as cricket creates 'links between nations of different religious persuasions' (Werbner, 1996: 95). Cricket is a masculine sport and, viewed as a male sport, reflects forms of male nationalism.

Despite the popularity of the national team, the support for domestic cricket is less evident and another trend is that those who play at the national level are often educated abroad (especially the captains) (Bandyopadhyay, 2007). In international cricket, views of the Pakistani cricket team often reflect wider views about Pakistani culture, such as religious fanaticism, cheating, and the view that Pakistan remains a pre-modern society; incidents such as the sudden death of Pakistan's coach Bob Woolmer during the 2007 World Cup, which created extensive rumours about the death, and the attack on 2 March 2009 on the Sri Lankan cricket team in a terrorist incident in Pakistan also reflect on the game. These high-profile incidents, alongside match-fixing scandals, have constantly put Pakistani cricket at the centre of several debates in the global game, and international matches are not currently played in Pakistan due to the perceived security threat. However, a constant in the game is that cricket in Pakistan has been a masculine sport that reflects nationalism and masculinity and the relationship is very strong (Werbner, 1996).

Emergence of women's cricket in Pakistan

Given the western view of Pakistan as a country that continues to have extreme power relations between men's and women's cricket, the existence of a women's cricket team often comes as a surprise. Women's cricket in Pakistan is wrongly considered a new sport, and this view exists even in established/published accounts. For example, Duncan (2013) suggests that women's cricket began in Pakistan in 1996, with the formation of the Pakistan Women's Cricket Council; however this is not the case. Women's cricket seems to date to the 1970s and the first governing body of the women's game was created in 1977 when the Pakistan Women's Cricket Association (PWCA) was formed at the Lahore College for Women. The first president of the organisation was the principal of the Lahore College for Women, suggesting a strong link between the college and the women's game. The extent to which the game was played by women is likely to have been quite limited, but from the outset the PWCA was in liaison with the BCCP. The PWCA was keen to inform the BCCP of its existence and to request equipment;

> I on behalf of the Pakistan Women's Cricket Association request you to kindly donate a complete set of cricket gear including cricket balls for the training and coaching camp (Hamid, October 15 1978)

This request for support is for a relatively small amount but demonstrates that the PWCA was keen to ensure that the BCCP was aware of its existence; and the BCCP did offer the support requested and was thanked for its support in subsequent correspondence (Hamid, 1979). In 1978 another school, the Lady MacLagon Girls High School, started cricket, and a national women's cricket tournament was started in 1979. In 1980 the PWCA invited an Indian team to tour, but this was rejected on the following grounds:

> Women's cricket in Pakistan is still in its infancy. It would, therefore, not be appropriate to face India at this moment or in the near future. Your request for exchange visits with India will be considered sometime in 1981 (Nasim, 1980).

Given that Indian women's cricket was also still relatively new, this rejection is interesting as the Indian women's organisation had extensive support from the IWCC and other nations at the outset. Yet it may signal power relations within the women's game with a small number of nations controlling the development of the women's game and marginalising of particular nations. The women's team continued to struggle for recognition, and in May 1981, a further correspondence with the BCCP requested affiliation:

> Sir, now the time has come that we should get the support by the board and at the end of this year we would like to invite a foreign team so that girls should get the confidence themselves that will only come if our girls play with a foreign team. I would be highly grateful if the affiliation is granted to PWCA.

This request for support was either ignored or negatively responded to as the BCCP was not forthcoming for support. There is no evidence to suggest at this time that the PWCA were in correspondence with women's cricket.

Gender relations within Pakistan are complex and violence against women is common. As mentioned in the context of India, violence against women impacts on gender relations and women's opportunities more broadly. The global gender gap index, which is used by the World Economic Forum to measure the scope and magnitude of gender inequity in different countries, placed Pakistan as 134th out of 135 countries (Hussain, 2013). This measure is based on four pillars: economic participation and opportunity, educational attainment, health and survival, and political empowerment. This demonstrates wider social issues that impact on women's ability to access leisure and sporting opportunities when power imbalances between men and women remain so extreme. Women's access to cricket cannot be considered in isolation to these wider national contexts. Arguably power relations between men and women and gender relations in national contexts are important to understanding the development of women's cricket.

The political and organisational instability in men's cricket has also been mirrored in the women's game as two organisations claim to govern the women's game. The Pakistan Women's Cricket Control Association (PWCCA) was formed in 1996 by Shaiza and Sharmeen Khan. The two sisters are daughters of a businessman and both were educated in England. The animosity between the PWCCA and the PWCA, both claiming to represent the game, led to the Pakistan Cricket Board (PCB) being asked to preside over the issue. The PCB decided that the PWCCA should be the governing body for cricket. Yet in 2003, Pakistan pulled out of the qualifying tournament due to visa issues and the continual perception that no one organisation had complete governance over the game. In 2005 as per the ICC mandate, which was part of the merger between IWCC and ICC, the PCB was required to take over the governance of the game and the PCB decided that instead of bringing together expertise from both existing groups into the PCB, neither organisation 'was fit' to run the women's game as part of the PCB and a fresh start was suggested (Khan and Khan, 2013). This approach ignored the key players and organisers in the women's existing organisations and demonstrates how established groups can shape the development of the game in particular ways that may not be supported by those in existing women's cricket organisations.

Khan, chair of the PCB at the time of the ICC mandate when the women's game came under the governance of the PCB, suggests that there was little overt resistance to women playing cricket. Currently, some women play in the hijab whereas others do not, and individual women are free to choose whether they wear the hijab or not. This choice seems to run contrary to the perceived, Western perception of sport, women and Islam, whereby people wrongly assume female Muslims are unable to participate in sport. Support for the women's game in Pakistan continues to be problematic and despite the merger the women's game has not always been at the forefront of PCB policies. August 2012 saw the first overt commitment to the game, the PCB offered 17 women central contracts demonstrating support for the women's game, although the amount of these is not thought to be enough to live off.

Wider support for the game is still mixed and the PCB ensures the security of the women's team by playing in secure locations. Playing in secure locations may be required because of wider security issues or because some still object to women playing cricket, and such need for protection could be viewed as being related to protection against violence for women who play the game, demonstrating a complex picture for females playing the game.

The development of women's cricket in Pakistan has been impacted on not only by wider gender relations between men and women but also by internal politics. Arguably the existence of the women's game and being part of the male established organisational body reflect wider civilising processes and functional democratisation between men and women, whereby power imbalances in the men's and women's game have lessened (but not equalised). Gender relations more broadly continue to be extremely unbalanced. It is perhaps not sociologically surprising that the women's game was developed through educational institutions, a similar pattern to the game in other national contexts. Education seems to be significant in the development of women's cricket; the women's game was developed in all female institutions, allowing some freedom for cricket to develop away from the established group. Yet in the Pakistan context the game struggled to gain recognition amongst political and organisational instability and continuing power imbalances between men and women which remain largely unequal. This, combined with infighting amongst female cricketers as an outsider group which lacked group cohesion, has continued to impact on the development of women's cricket. These issues, alongside further changes that were part of the ICC mandate which effectively put the PCB in control of the women's game, have meant that the social processes involved in the development of the women's game have been turbulent.

The dominance of England more broadly in the outsiders' national characters in the game and the view that the English women's team is the most established team in the women's game are reflected in a recent expression by the Pakistan captain who, after beating England in England, explains that it was the most memorable match of her career. This demonstrates pride in beating the mother country at its own game, reflecting a type of national pride often reflected in men's cricket, but also a realisation that the standard of cricket played is at the global level and that one can compete at the top levels of the women's game (Hussain, 2013). Whilst these relations might be important to players, in reality, the significance of women's team beating England to wider issues of national identity is much less than that of the national expression of elation when the men's team is successful. This alongside continuing inequities between men and women and political instability and lack of state monopoly over violence towards women continues to position the women's game as inferior to the men's game and demonstrates how the nation state, power, gender relations and women's access to sport and leisure are inextricably linked.

Cricket and gender relations in New Zealand

The New Zealand Cricket Council (NZCC) was formed in 1894, although cricket matches had been played since colonial times and matches were featured as part of bank holidays and festivals. The first men's game was recorded in 1832, with initial matches being played by colonists and played by men. Initial involvement of women was limited to being spectators, and a book published by William Outwaite in 1833 entitled *The Ladies Guide to Cricket, by a Lover of Both* (cited in Ryan, 2004: 95) suggests that women's knowledge of the game was limited and that women needed men to explain the rules for women to enjoy the game, and the rather tongue-in-cheek title suggests that women were not taken seriously as spectators.

The first reference to women playing cricket is in Greyton on New Year's Day in 1867 (Ryan, 2004). The next recorded match is much later in 1886, suggesting a sporadic approach to the women's game. Some clubs are reported to have existed in the early 1890s and girls' cricket was played in schools. Yet the game was firmly rooted as a male sport. It reflected male values and reinforced notions of masculinity, and women playing were ridiculed. Medical objections were also evident to women playing; like elsewhere, concern about women's biology was used as a way to ensure that girls and women were considered unsuitable for the game:

> However fascinating cricket may be a sport amongst girls, it undoubtedly favours an ungainly gait, a stop, a asymmetry, contracted shoulders and irregular awkward movement of the arms (cited in Ryan, 2004: 96).

The NZCC, like all initial national organisations, comprised only males and they did not demonstrate any support for the women's game; however this is not unusual. There were strong objections to women playing cricket, and these objections seem to centre around the view that cricket was not suited to women, and medical discourses were used to enforce this view. Despite this, some elite schools did have girls' cricket, but those that played out of the safety of the school system and in the public seem to have been dismissed and ridiculed. The introduction and subsequent development of cricket in schools and the sport curricula seem essential to ensure access to the sport by women and girls more broadly.

In 1928 the formation of an area cricket association in Auckland helped to develop cricket for girls and women; Christchurch developed an organisation in 1929 and this was developed predominantly by hockey players. Otago set it up in 1930 and Wellington developed an organisation in 1932, these organisations set the path for the formation of the New Zealand Women's Cricket Council (NZWCC) in 1934. England approached New Zealand to consider a tour to follow after the inaugural trip to Australia and it seems this prompted the formation of the NZWCC. This allowed for the first tour and England toured in 1935. The lack of experience in the national side and the new teams was evident as New Zealand lost. Support for the tour came from Dame Elizabeth Knox Gilmer, daughter of a former prime minister who was a supporter of cricket, and she paid for England to stay in Wellington in 1935. The NZCC did not support the team and financial support came from players, fundraising or one-off charitable donations. At this time there was still very little cricket being played in New Zealand and standards of the game had not developed fully. Objection to the sport was predominantly through ridicule; as Whitelaw, a player at the time, notes in the 1936 Women's Cricket magazine: 'England visit in the masculine quarter the games, had more or less, been regarded as a joke' (Hutton Whitelaw, 1936: 10). Concern about propriety was also an issue for women playing as uniform and dress were discussed and it was stressed that female cricketers had a responsibility to dress respectably (Whitelaw, 1936). Attempts to govern the game proved difficult; the game continued to struggle to develop, there were few players, and until 1957 there were still only around 1,000 players. It was not until 1954 that the team members were able to tour and they visited England, although there were problems in funding the tour, and not all players were able to travel. The extent of this problem is discussed in the magazine of the England Women's Cricket Association (EWCA) as being an ongoing problem for not just the NZWCC but for many national governing bodies of this time (Women's Cricket Association, 1954). New Zealand was instrumental in the global organisation of the game and was a member of the IWCC from the outset in 1958.

Despite the lack of support at the start of the game New Zealand was the first country to merge the men's and women's cricket boards, in 1992, and support was more forthcoming. In the New Zealand context, this merger led to greater interdependency between the two groups and appears to have supported the development of women's cricket. However, ongoing issues relate to the semi-professional status of some teams compared to the amateur status of others; as discussed in Chapter 5, the New Zealand women's team remains predominantly amateur and the development of the women's game is arguably impacted by these ongoing financial issues.

South African cricket and gender relations

Africans were reported to be involved in cricket from 1862, with the first African Cricket Club founded in 1869. Cricket in South Africa, as elsewhere, was framed as a form of nationalism, with matches in the 1860s between the mother country and colonial-born cricketers suggesting that cricket can symbolise struggles between the mother country and colonial rule. The role of cricket in these debates about colonialism was critical and forms of nationalism were represented in these matches, but these were solely about the nation, men and masculinity. The South African Cricket Association (SACA) was formed in 1890. Women cricketers, like black cricketers, are not as well documented in the history of the game and have been ignored in historical accounts of the game (Odendaal, 2011), a reminder that history is often written by the established group and that in certain contexts the outsider group is rendered invisible by establishment accounts of the game. Research on cricket in South Africa has focused predominantly on men's cricket, and issues of race and South African politics (Allen, 2010).

Women's initial role in cricket in South Africa seems to be as supporters of the game, and cricket events were social occasions with extensive social networking opportunities. Women were very much part of the cricket scene (Odendaal, 2011). They were encouraged to support the game but within certain boundaries of acceptability, that is, with suitable attire and in line with broader notions of acceptable femininity.

The first known report of women playing is in 1888 and women and men played matches, although men would 'handicap' themselves by playing left-handed, the assumption being that women needed help to compete with men. In 1893 a proposal was put forward to the annual general meeting of the Western Province Cricket Club to allow women to be admitted as members, but this was rejected, demonstrating the extent to which gender relations ensured that men (mainly white men) were able to define what access women had to private clubs and that they had the power to define membership.

Women were playing in other established clubs such as the Wanderers in Johannesburg and Ramblers Club in Bloemfontein and these teams did play seriously (Odendaal, 2011). Cricket was played in girls' schools that were modelled on the British public school system for girls and the ideology of sport for girls was part of the postwar Anglicisation of South Africa, comprising the idea that cricket could teach girls skills such as loyalty to country and moral virtue. The first black women's club was thought to be formed in 1909 (Odendaal, 2011).

Despite women playing, cricket was firmly considered to be a manly activity that reflected colonial ideologies, such as the belief that cricket was a male sport that enhanced masculinity and gentle-manliness. Women generally played on private grounds, and they did not challenge male spaces (Odendaal, 2011). In the 1920s many schools appointed British physical education (PE) teachers and there was a renewed focus on girls' involvement in sport; these schools were modelled on British girls' public schools and thus reflected British attitudes towards girls and sport, thus encouraging cricket. In 1920s the Peninsula Girls' Schools Games Union was formed, with a president. Much later, in 1932 the Peninsula Ladies' Cricket Club (PLCC) was formed, and because there was no organisation in South Africa, the club was affiliated to the EWCA. As the game lacked an international organisation, the EWCA took responsibility for organising the women's game. Interest in the game more broadly and in the EWCA can also be seen in the fact that the magazine of EWCA was sent to South Africa from the 1930s. The PLCC were instrumental in the development of the women's game and women played against the men's team, demonstrating some level of interdependency between men's and women's cricket at this stage, although there is little discussion about what the men thought about the women's team at this time.

During World War II, like elsewhere women's cricket declined, but a revival in the 1950s meant that several provinces were playing cricket and an interprovincial competition was created in 1952–53. The South African and Rhodesian Women's Cricket Association (SARWCA) was formed in 1952, although some of the provinces had organisations before this date. A tournament against provinces was created in which all provinces played each other; there was a trophy and also the annual general meetings of SARWCA were held during this time. It seems from the records that men were instrumental in the development of the women's game, more so than in other cricketing nations and one member of the steering committee was the test cricketer Eric Rowan. South Africa was a part of the founding members of the IWCC in 1958; this is despite the country not yet having played a test game, demonstrating differing levels of acceptance in the IWCC and the ICC.

South Africa played its first international test game against England in 1960 and played four test matches. The first test match was played at Port Elizabeth. The standard of the South African players was of a reasonable level and the match ended in a draw. Male umpires were used for the test matches and prominent test grounds were utilised. Most of those spectating were men; this is interesting as the press reports were also complimentary, with a press report stating of the English women: 'Their batting has character and technically it is equal to much of what one would find among our top-class men players' (Odendaal, 2011: 126). This support for women's cricket quickly declined after the tour, as did the numbers playing, and one reason cited is financial issues. There were few registered players, and by 1966 there was a suggestion that there were only 130 women playing. There were also concerns being raised by other countries about the suitability of other countries playing against South Africa. For example, when Jamaica joined the IWCC it refused to tour South Africa or to let South Africa tour Jamaica (*WCA Yearbook*, 1970). This reflects broader issues in cricket as South Africa was largely banned from international sport during Apartheid politics. It was subsequently excluded from the Women's World Cup in 1973. Some unofficial tours to South Africa continued, but in effect South African tours and cricket declined.

In 1990 the African National Congress (ANC) encouraged the South African Cricket Board (SACB) to form a United Cricket Board of South Africa (UCBSA) in 1991. This was done so that international cricket could be resumed. Later the South African Women's Cricket Association (SAWCA) was formed in 1996 and it replaced the previously white-only SARWCA.

South African cricket continues to be affected by ongoing race relations in the country. These issues have not received much academic attention in women's sport but may need further consideration as South Africa was instrumental in the development of women's cricket and it was part of the formation of the IWCC in 1958 (as discussed in Chapter 4).

Cricket and gender relations in West Indies

The West Indies is a multinational conglomeration of Caribbean countries that represent several nations; therefore a West Indian cricket team is a peculiarity in world sport (Malcolm, 2013). The first reference to cricket in the West Indian press was in 1806. At the time the military was heavily involved in matches and involvement in the early forms of cricket is well documented (Malcolm, 2013). Initially the military teams played between themselves, but during slavery black men were encouraged to use their free time to do approved activities which were viewed as civilised, and cricket was an approved activity. The process of cricket beginning with the military demonstrates the link between cricket and masculinity; cricket was played by men and it reflected a type of English masculinity strongly linked with colonialism. With time, slaves began to play in cricket games within military matches. Malcolm (2013) notes how cricketing roles of black males in the early days of cricket mirrored the experience of working class professionals in English cricket. Black males often took on the position of bowlers, a position which was considered lower in status than batting. Cricket more broadly played an important role in the Caribbean context in defining types of masculinity; the game allowed the white male community to continue to demonstrate loyalty to the crown. White men playing in heat also proved that the tropics did not undermine the physical capabilities of white men as environmental determinism had suggested at the time.

Once slavery was abolished, the game had a key role in distancing the 'elite' groups, and issues of race and race relations continued to influence the development of the game. It was factors such as these that, according to Malcolm (2013), resulted in cricket in the Caribbean spreading extensively in the second half of the nineteenth century, and playing was organised on codes of social ranking, wealth, colour and occupation. However, in all cases the game was a male sport reflecting particular types of masculinity and playing a role in racial segregation and power struggles in the game.

Whether cricket was played in non-white clubs or white-only clubs, it was a male sport; there is no mention of women playing cricket. Men's cricket tours began in 1895. Initially these were white-only teams but there was some recognition that this limited the talent and ability of teams. Increasingly black players were selected but in selected positions as bowlers. Selection committees and organisers of the game were predominantly white and the roles of batsmen and captaincy continued to be limited to whites only, as a firm established and outsider figuration was formed.

Although white West Indians viewed the game as theirs, black West Indians were involved and played the game as well. In this context, cricket became a form of resistance, and it came to be viewed as being a sport that 'challenges, undermines, and finally refashions imperial cultural practices towards being an expression of political autonomy by the colonized' (cited in Mustafa, 2013: 330). Black nationalism and the demand for social reform were also reflected in a variety of social processes and these can be reflected in cricket and its development. However, as Beckles (1998) suggests, neither colonialism nor nationalism sought to problematise the issue of patriarchy and masculinity in the game. As black cricket clubs developed and were supported by businessmen, this enabled cricket clubs to develop the game largely away from and separate from white organisational control. Similar to the Indian cricket context, the financing of black teams was essential to the development of club cricket, which subverted the game from a white gentleman's game to a game in which colonised people could assert power and authority. Early struggles in the game centred on race and class, not on issues of gender as Beckles (1998) illustrates; a letter published in the *Dominica Star* on 17 May 1969 stated:

> Black power leaders have urged West Indians to "throw off the white Imperialist culture and adopt Black African Ways" . . . isn't there a good African game our young men could play in the Botanical Gardens on Sunday (cited in Beckles, 1998: 119)

The perception of cricket and games more broadly seems to illustrate an established and outsider figuration in which the established group was fragmented around issues of race and class and women were positioned firmly as outsiders in the West Indian game. Like other activities in nineteenth-century West Indies such as political leadership and corporate management, cricket was not considered suitable for women (Beckles, 1998). Here we see the establishment of an established and outsider figuration in which the established group clearly has a monopolisation on physical and ideological resources that position the men's game as symbolising racial and colonial struggles in relation to men. This, alongside strong established behavioural codes about gender and patriarchy, positioned women as supporters of male cricket and critically in their role in supporting their husbands and sons playing (Beckles, 1998). Whilst 'black men and white men jostled for position in relation to the historic rights of ownership, women have remained silent' (Beckles, 1998: 119).

Emergence of women's cricket

Women were not involved in the early days of the West Indian game and there is little evidence of women playing on the islands. It was in Jamaica that the game for women was first played and the Jamaica Women's Cricket Association (JWCA) was the first to form in 1966 (Heyhoe Flint and Rheinberg, 1976). The emergence of the organisation came from around 30–40 women who were interested in the game. A league competition was developed and in 1967 a team toured Trinidad. Monica Taylor, a prominent businesswomen and campaigner (Beckles, 1998), was instrumental in the organisation of playing cricket for women. She has been a prominent campaigner, more broadly illustrating a relationship between political involvement and women's sport involvement (perhaps similar to the Australian context).

According to Beckles (1998), this was a significant time in the social history of West Indian cricket. Women had played an important part in the anti-colonialism movement more broadly and their move into cricket signalled a shift in wider power relations between men and women. A league competition was set up in 1967 and a tour suggested to Trinidad and Tobago, which prompted the formation of a Trinidad and Tobago Women's Cricket Association in 1967. The timing of this is significant; as Beckles (1998) indicates, it was after a transformation in West Indian cricket more broadly in which the black nationalist and socialist movement had taken control over political resources, and also there had been a transformation of cricket in which blacks were able to control the national team. This shift in broader power relations and race relations enabled a space for women's cricket as part of wider shifts in power relations between the sexes which saw a reimagining of aspects of West Indian culture.

Teams began to emerge and these were often sponsored by companies that supported the team by giving playing equipment. Jamaica affiliated to the IWCC in 1968, only a year after cricket was played on the island. This is significant as it signals once again the position of the IWCC in that they had to allow most national governing bodies the opportunity to join, despite cricket being such a new sport. In 1970 an England representative team visited Jamaica and test match cricket was played, with a substantial amount of support and spectators, with 6,000 attending the match at Sabina Park (Heyhoe Flint and Rheinberg, 1976). Press reports were also generally positive; one reporter in the *Sunday Gleaner* reported, 'Some of the catching I have seen by women of both sides should be an object lesson for the butter fingered male cricketers (cited in Duncan, 2013: 89). However, some responses and media reports did focus on women's appearance and 'shapely legs', illustrating a sexist approach to media reporting (Beckles, 1998). Women's cricket in the Caribbean was very competitive, with leagues, trophies and knockout competitions (Heyhoe Flint and Rheinberg, 1976).

Links between the Caribbean countries and England continued with six players travelling to the UK to play in the 1970 cricket week. This demonstrates the role England cricket played in the development of the women's game. . During this time, regional competition was also increasing. The fact that some women were able to travel to play in England suggests that the women who travelled were able to afford to travel and support themselves for the costs associated with the travel must have been extensive.

In 1971 Jamaica, Trinidad and Tobago, and England played a triangular test series and Trinidad and Tobago beat England, suggesting that despite the infancy of the game, women must have been competent and this probably suggests that women had been playing for some time even in the absence of a formal organisation. At the first World Cup in 1973 in England, both Jamaica and Trinidad and Tobago competed, albeit as separate countries. In 1973, Barbados joined the IWCC and then in 1974 Grenada started playing. Given the amount of cricket that was being played in the Caribbean and its fairly rapid development, in 1975 a Caribbean Women's Cricket Federation (CWCF) was formed, which created a regional framework for women's cricket. As the CWCF tours were organised to India and England, the CWCF continued to develop separate from its male counterparts.

The men's West Indies Cricket Board (WICB) did not demonstrate support or interest in the women's game. This is symptomatic of the established and outsider figuration, which in the West Indian context seems quite pronounced; the emergence of evidence for women playing cricket on the islands shows that the women's game developed much later than in other contexts. Cricket firmly reflected a type of masculinity in the Caribbean, and within the men's game there have been extensive power struggles in its development. There is little evidence of correspondence between men and women cricketers (players) at the outset of the game. However, cricket in the Caribbean for girls and women seems to follow a slightly different pattern in that the game was not played in schools/colleges; rather it was the emergence of clubs that then took cricket to girls' schools. Cricket clubs for women seem to have been supported by prominent male cricketers; the coach to the 1971 Jamaica side was a male and a member of the Marylebone Cricket Club (MCC), illustrating that male support was not withheld or rejected and suggesting some level of support, perhaps indicating differing notions of mutual identification amongst male cricketers. Male umpires often supported events and coached women to play the game. The notion of cricket and masculinity is so ingrained in that women's involvement in the game has struggled for recognition (Beckles, 1998). Some men have clearly supported the women's game on an individual basis. However on a formal level there seemed little interaction between the men's and women's national governing bodies and some evidence suggests that there has been resistance to women using main grounds and facilities in the West Indies (Beckles, 1998). Media reports of the women's game remain minimal and few are aware of the women's game (Beckles, 1998).

Other examples of exclusion have come from decisions to not employ female coaches and to not invite women players, including those women who play for their country, to official functions or cricket events. Many test venues such as Sabina Park have male-only bars; such strategies of exclusion are mirrored in the MCC and at Lord's in England. A lack of financial support also impacted on women's cricket, and fans expected women cricketers to compete at the same level as the men without support. West Indian female players themselves often identify closely with established male players, choosing male role models and mimicking male styles of play, a consequence no doubt of their outsider status. The WICB has had no strategic involvement in women's cricket and it did not merge until 2005 as part of the ICC mandate. The legacy of nationalism that positioned cricket in wider struggles impacted strongly and enabled men to monopolise the sport. Women cricketers remain outsiders in what continues to be an established and outsider figuration with substantial power imbalances.

Women, cricket and gender relations in Sri Lanka

Cricket in Sri Lanka (formerly known as Ceylon) has a long history dating to 1832. Sri Lanka became a British colony in 1802, so it is thought that cricket was played on the island from this date (Little, 2012). Despite this long history of cricket on the island, only in 1982 did Sri Lanka play test cricket after being granted test status that year. Like in other contexts, cricket was brought to the island by the British and early reports suggest that the game was played predominantly by British soldiers, schoolmasters and those working for the Empire as administrators. Cricket was an integral part of English language schools and it came to be played by an emerging middle-class indigenous population. These schools were for boys and it was boys who were involved in the game. There are no early records of the game being played by women on the island. The first male club was formed in 1832 and this was the Colombo Cricket Club; this club was formed by the British after a notice appeared in the *Colombo Journal* that invited 'gentlemen who may be inclined towards forming a cricket club to meet at the library at 2 'o' clock' (cited in Mangan, 2010: 426). Here the reference to gentlemen also signals a class and race issue as the club was predominantly for British residents.

Sri Lanka played a role in the development of cricket more broadly as the location of the island meant it was often a stopping point between Australia and England (Little, 2012). Matches on the island initially were played by Europeans; it was not until 1890 that the Australian team played against a team that defined itself as being Ceylonese (Little, 2012). The Colts Cricket Club, which was formed much later than the Colombo Cricket Club, was established in 1873 and was made up of Ceylon's mixed-race Eurasian population, still not incorporating indigenous populations. Cricket became established in the boys' school system as manliness was emphasised through cricket. Schools such as Trinity College in Kandy for children of elite families emphasised leadership through cricket and saw cricket as a way of instilling discipline in boys as it was viewed more broadly as a civilising mission; many of these headmasters were from England and adopted English public school systems, including games in their schools (Mangan, 2010). There is some evidence that women played cricket at the Nondescripts Cricket Club (NCC), a club established for all ethnic groups in 1888, although such matches are not recorded and are difficult to verify.

At this time sporting stopovers on the island were gendered and involved male teams. The Australian women's cricket team did stop in Sri Lanka in 1937, but they did not play cricket like their male counterparts due to a lack of opposition (Little, 2012). Later in 1948, an England women's team did stop in Colombo on the way to Australia. Joy (1950) recalls how the England women's team were met by the Board of Control for Cricket in Ceylon on 1 November. The women then played a match on Tamil Union Ground. This is potentially significant as it demonstrates that some development in the women's game took place between 1937 and 1948, albeit amongst white European women. The England team played against an All-Ceylon XI and this included several European women and a 'dear little Ceylonese fifteen-year-old school girl' (Joy, 1950: 62). The match was watched by 7,000 spectators; this number of supporters may reflect the novelty value as this is the first-recorded match on the island. After the match, the England women went to the prestigious Colombo Cricket Club, which was an exclusive European Club, for a cocktail party. Joy's (1950: 64) reflections of the match and the indigenous population illustrate a perception of race and relations widely held at the time, as she praises 'the Ceylonese girls, and their natural aptitude for cricket, with their quick eye and loose wrists, characteristics of their race'.

There are few records about women playing cricket; this may be because the game was so closely related to masculinity that women did not play or it may signal that women played away from public view. The violent civil war that has been an integral part of the history of the island and the relationship between physicality, masculinity and nationalism may have impacted on women's access to opportunities to play the game. Women have always been encouraged to support the men's game, and when Sri Lanka won the World Cup in 1996, the country celebrated extensively and the win seems to reflect a type of nationalism that largely transcends the ethnic tensions between Tamil and Sinhalese populations and the long-standing violence between the two groups. There is not enough scope here to discuss this violence and civil war and its impact on men's cricket other than to say that ethnic tensions, power relations and nationalism are tensions in Sri Lankan men's cricket (Roberts, 2010). Nevertheless, cricket is a site where 'questions of nation, identity, desire and agency are played out' (Perera, 2000). Although Perera (2000) talks about the complexity of Sri Lankan cricket and national identities, gender is not addressed or fully discussed in these accounts, as women themselves support the Sri Lanka national team, which is the male team, and this support is in reflection of a national identity that is centred on a masculine identification with the nation.

The dominance of men's cricket in Sri Lanka and the relationship between cricket and masculinity and national identity has severely impacted on women's involvement (at least publicly). As Dunning (1999) illustrates, war (and whatever shape this may take) often impacts on gender relations and the equalisation of gender relations is less likely to develop in this context. Official discussions of the Sri Lankan game make little reference to the women's game; for example, Robert's (2006) *Essaying Cricket, Sri Lanka and Beyond* does not mention women playing at all. However in relation to cricket, an established and outsider figuration between men's and women's cricket seems largely absent as women do not appear to have been involved in cricket at all. A formal organisation for the women's cricket did not emerge until 1997 when the Women's Cricket Association of Sri Lanka (WCASL) was formed and in the same year the WCASL became a member of the IWCC.

Cricket for women in Sri Lanka is presently run by the national governing body Sri Lanka Cricket, as part of the ICC mandate for merging of governing bodies. The team has developed into a competitive cricket side and in 2010 full-time contracts were given to players, but the game remains in the shadow of men's cricket, a reflection of national identity and national pride.

Cricket and gender relations in Holland and Ireland

In the nations discussed above the role of nation states, national identity, masculinity and cricket are key in understanding the emergence and development of women's cricket. In Holland and Ireland a slightly different picture emerges in the development of women's cricket that is worth consideration. Holland was a part of the founding countries that formed the IWCC in 1958. Although it did not actually attend the first meeting, it did attend by proxy and is recognised as one of the founding countries from the outset. Ireland joined the IWCC in 1987. Interestingly neither country has ICC full membership in men's cricket, and they are both associate members, which is defined as being

> the governing bodies for cricket of a country recognised by the ICC, or countries associated for cricket purposes, or a geographical area, which does not qualify as a Full Member, but where cricket is firmly established and organised (38 Members). (ICC)

Men's cricket was played in Holland from 1790s but early matches did not follow MCC rules and thus cricket was not taken seriously by the cricketing elite and the ICC, which were elitist in their approach to who could play international cricket. The game was not played or followed extensively in Holland.

Women's cricket in Holland appears to date to around 1930, with a club that developed in Haarlem and, in a not-dissimilar context to other countries, those playing appear to have had strong links to hockey (Duncan, 2013). An official association, the Nederlandse Dames Cricket Bond, was formed in 1934 with league cricket being played. This date is significantly earlier than in other now-more-established cricket nations and is also around the time of the first international match. Also at this time men's cricket does not seem to have been played extensively, so the relationship between cricket, masculinity and nationalism seems much weaker than in other national contexts. The Dutch organisation seemed to have had strong links to the EWCA and the AWCC as Australia toured in 1937 as part of their wider tour to England, but matches were played on matting wickets as the soil and pitches were not suitable (Duncan, 2013). One of the problems with cricket in Holland was the lack of pitches; pitches were bumpy and not of a standard for international matches and facilities were few and far between. As men's cricket was not played there were no facilities available for women to use, and no established organisation to be able to play. Cricket seemed to have been suspended during the war but re-emerged in 1949, when a league was developed and links between the England and Holland teams seemed to have continued. England toured Holland in 1952 and Holland came to England. The first official EWCA tour to Holland was in 1959. The links between the two countries and the fact that cricket was at its strongest during this era might explain why Holland was involved at the outset of the IWCC's formation in 1958, as England was instrumental in the development of the IWCC. The association continued to have strong links to the EWCA, but it appears the organisation was disbanded in the 1970s after a period of decline.

It was the involvement of men's cricket that seems to have enabled the women's game to re-emerge and male cricketers promoted the women's game in the late 1970s in their cricket magazines. The level of interdependency between male and female cricketers in Holland seem to be in contrast to that in other countries; as men's cricket was a marginal sport in Holland, men and women cricketers were interdependent on one another for survival. They had to pool resources for survival and men did not have such a monopolisation on the resources of the game. In addition the game was not as strongly linked to either masculinity or nationalism as it was elsewhere. The men's team also played England women for publicity, demonstrating a different approach to issues of cricket and masculinity from that seen elsewhere. Women's cricket re-emerged in 1984 and the team made its international debut against New Zealand 26 years after being part of the IWCC; the team's involvement in the game continues albeit at low levels of the game. Interestingly in recent years, the support given by men to women's cricket in Holland has declined, indicating perhaps that the men's game is going through a period of nationalism and as part of this it might be increasingly being considered a sport that reflects nationality, masculinity. Lack of facilities is also an ongoing issue for Dutch women. In 2007, the women's national side played its first test match against South Africa. The women have been more successful of late. In 2011 Holland won the European 50-over and T20 championships. The team finished seventh in the World Cup qualifying tournament in Bangladesh in November 2011.

Men's cricket in Ireland was generally played by the British military and aristocracy and it was not diffused down to rural areas, thus the game has not had significant support. The first-recorded women's match in Ireland is in 1884, against a men's team in Strabane, in which the women are reported to have won (Duncan, 2013). In 1890, the first all-women's match was played in Cork.

In Ireland too, clubs supporting the women's game existed in Southern Ireland and a Leinster Women's Cricket Union organised cricket in the Dublin area. Cricket was played at the girls' schools, with competition between schools, and an Irish School Girls' XI toured England in 1908. There was no main organising body for the women's game, and there must have been some opposition as at Trinity College women cricketers were banned from using the men's ground at College Park.

By the 1970s, the game seems to have gone into decline; then it re-emerged in the 1980s with the formation of the Irish Women's Cricket Union (IWCU), and Ireland competed in a tournament in Holland in 1982. Cricket was played in Ulster and Munster and new leagues were created. Internationally Ireland played a three-match one-day series against Australia in 1987. Although Ireland lost against such a competent side, it was later involved in the 1988 World Cup. This was far in advance of an Irish men's team competing internationally, again illustrating some differences in the diffusion of men's and women's cricket and the emergence of the women's game in lesser cricket-playing nations. Ireland played its first test against Pakistan in 2000. Women's cricket was amalgamated into the Irish Cricket Union in 2003, before the ICC mandate. The Irish senior side competes in the Leinster men's league and has gained promotion on a regular basis. Ireland has also competed in the England and Wales Cricket Board (ECB) LV County Championships since 2009. It is interesting that the team plays in the English ECB tournament, as it is unusual for a country to develop its national team by utilising the structure in another country to develop a national side. Recently Ireland has twice won the European Championships – in 2005 and 2009, and has started to become more dominant in international cricket tournaments.

Cricket in Ireland and Holland have developed differently from the main cricket nations; both were part of the early international organisation for the women's game, despite a lack of quality cricket being played. In these nation states the established outsider figuration between men and women's cricket was not as marked, and relations between male and female cricketers were more interdependent; however the lack of structure and facilities in counties which did not embrace cricket as a national sport impacted on the development of men's and women's cricket. The fact that these two nations joined the IWCC demonstrates that unlike the ICC which had strict guidelines for who could join (not just based on playing standards but other issues about the monopolisation of who should play cricket) the international organisation, the IWCC, were more inclusive in which nations they included, arguably a result of their outsider status.

Concluding thoughts

There are some distinct patterns that emerge in tracing the social processes involved in the emergence and development of women's cricket that are worth noting. Whilst not oversimplifying the process of diffusion, there are four distinct issues that arise in considering the international development of cricket in different nations. Firstly, cricket was diffused as a male sport that reflected a type of English masculinity and nationalism, and at the time of diffusion, cricket was firmly established as a male sport. Secondly, although the diffusion process has developed differently with differing patterns of acceptance and resistance, in all nations discussed above (apart from Ireland and Holland), cricket came to reflect a form of nationalism and masculinity that often was part of wider race, class and issues of power in relation to colonialism but these struggles tended to reinforce gender relations and patriarchy more by positioning cricket as a sport for men than reflecting a type of national identity and often colonial struggles. Thirdly, women supported the game of cricket, either as spectators or through supporting significant others; women are clearly part of the 'nation' that identifies with cricket as a form of nationalism. Fourthly, in each case discussed, an established and outsider figuration emerges; the power balances at the outset of women taking up the game in each country represents an established and outsider figuration with marked differences in terms of power relations, in which men are able from the outset to monopolise key resources. These resources are in relation to physicality (how suited women and men are physically to the game of cricket), ideologies in relation to the concept that cricket is a male sport that reinforces a type of national masculinity and, finally, in relation to organisational networks, in which men's governing bodies comprised the first governance of the game in each context, setting the rules of the game (literally and metaphorically).In all the countries discussed women's organisations emerge as separate from men's governing bodies without access to any of the key resources. In the case of Ireland and Holland a different pattern of established and outsider relations emerges where the lack of relationship between cricket masculinity and the nation mean that men's cricket has a marginal position. This means that men and women cricketers are more interdependent but that a general lack of resources and interest in cricket demonstrates a different struggle for recognition as a minor sport for men and women.

In each context, tracing the long-term social processes involved in the development of the men's and women's game is critical in understanding how women's cricket developed in relation to men's cricket, charting shifting power relations through the process of functional democratisation. An emerging pattern is the formation of established and outsider figurations in which power is extremely unbalanced; however other social processes, such as women's increasing access to public, political and educational opportunities, ensure a shift in power relations between the sexes, which includes greater interdependence and mutual understanding. That is, through the process of merging of male and female cricket organisations, which is discussed in the following chapter, clearly influencing women's access to cricket.

In tracing the development of women's cricket in different nation states, it is worth quoting Dunning (1999: 226) here at length as he discusses gender relations more broadly as this is important to the analysis presented in this chapter:

> Relations between males and females are fundamentally affected by the character and overall structure of the society in which they are lived. The form of economy, for example whether it takes one or another variant of the capitalist or socialist types, together with the society's level of economic development are clearly of significance in this regard. So is the position of the society in relation to others and the degree to which its intersocietal relations are warlike or peaceful.

Thus in considering the current gender relations and context of women's cricket in each of the nation states, there are significant issues which seem to have impacted on women's access to cricket. These are the positions of women more broadly in a society, for example, the extent to which women have access to educational opportunities, the extent to which the state has control over physical and sexual violence towards women and women's access to political voice (i.e. voting). These relations between males and females affect women's access to sport, and cricket more broadly. Thus, Dunning (1999) later suggests that the specific state of gender relations in a society may reflect the trajectory of that society's stage within a civilising process, and thus the support for women's cricket in a specific society may further reflect a type of civilising process in which the direction is towards equalisation. But there are variations in this regard and gender relations are also impacted on by globalisation more broadly in which discourses of equality and women's right have influenced through policies, NGOs and global human rights movements that continue to insist on better rights for girls and women, and increasingly these organisations signal the role of sport in reflecting wider power balances between men and women. In the following chapter I consider the international development of women's cricket, and international governing bodies and their influence on the emergence of women's cricket as a global game.

4
Women's Cricket, International Governance and Organisation of the Global Game

In Chapter 3, the emergence of women's cricket in a variety of national contexts was discussed: In particular the focus was how and why women's cricket emerged and what social processes were involved in the development of the game, drawing on figurational sociology as a framework for exploring the social processes and emergence of established and outsider figurations in specific national contexts. In this chapter, the international governance and the organisation of women's cricket as a global game are discussed, focusing on the social processes that enabled the emergence of a global governing body and the subsequent developments in the structures governing women's cricket. Since its formation in 1909, the International Cricket Council (ICC) has been the governing body of men's cricket. This organisation was originally controlled by England and Australia and it was an elitist organisation that influenced the development of men's cricket according to particular values and social habituses (closely linked to race and class relations more broadly).

In women's cricket, the global organisation of the game has been distinctly different and the purpose of this chapter is to discuss global issues in the women's game, highlighting the organisation and codification of women's cricket and the emergence of an international governing body, the International Women's Cricket Council (IWCC) in 1958. The chapter then goes on to consider the struggles of the organisation to develop global governance of the game, exploring how this is part of a broader issue relating to a consequence of being an outsider group within an established and outsider figuration. Secondly, the national case studies of the merging of men's and women's national governing bodies in Australia and England are explored to consider the processes of merging national organisations as part of wider discussions about gender equity and the social conditions that enabled the merging of two organisations considering broader issues and developments in women's sport and issues of equity more broadly.

The figurational concept of game models, alongside the theory of established and outsider relations, is used in this chapter to consider the nature of interdependence in global organisations. Game models illustrate how power exists in all human relationships in an attempt to demonstrate 'such power balances, not as extraordinary but as everyday occurrences' (Elias, 1978: 74). Game models illustrate the fluidity of power relations between groups and also avoid considering one group as all powerful. The relational element of game models is significant for understanding the nature of power relations and the unintended social processes. The more elaborate game models that Elias presents are complex and demonstrate how in social relations between a number of people or groups, it is impossible for one person to control the game or anticipate what might occur next. Elias suggests that once the game gets too disorganised, then smaller groups begin to coexist in the game and two-tier figurations emerge. These models clearly identify how no one player can influence the outcome of the game; thus the game model approach is described by Quilley and Loyal (2005: 821) as demonstrating

> how, as the number of players grows, the pattern of interdependency between individuals increased and power ratios between players tends to decline. This is the simplest theoretical expression of Elias' notion of functional democratization – that other things being equal, greater complexity in social and economic life leads to a lessening of power ratios.

One of the benefits of Elias' game models is the way in which he is able to demonstrate the polyvalent nature of power. This approach differs from more contemporary sociological theories about power, as it avoids the tendency to think about power and power balances as static. The concept is adopted in the first section of this chapter to consider the power relations that exist in the global women's game considering the complexity of the players involved.

The formation and development of the IWCC

The first discussions about the formation of an international governing body for women's cricket appear in the records of the England Women's Cricket Association (EWCA) in 1954, in which it is stated that it was suggested by members of the EWCA that an international women's cricket council be formed (Whitehorn, 1956). The context of this suggestion to form an international governance for the game is critical, as it is after World War II (WWII) (when the women's game saw a decline internationally), but this is significant in considering broader changes in mutual power relations between men and women, in which women gained access to public life more fully during WWII. Despite international tours being played from 1934, these tours were centrally organised by the respective national governing bodies, which whilst challenging financially had enabled international women's cricket to emerge. However by 1954, there had only been the 1934 tour of Australia and New Zealand by England, the return 1937 tour when Australia toured England and the 1951 Australia tour to England and a 1952 tour by Holland to England, although the tour was not an official international match but rather to develop links and cricket between Holland and England. The New Zealand cricketers were due to tour England in 1954. Thus by 1954, international women's cricket was still sporadic, hampered by WWII and also by the finances of national governing bodies.

It was not until 1956 that a draft constitution was developed by the EWCA, which was instrumental in suggesting the development of an international organisation. A draft constitution was sent to Australia, Holland, New Zealand and South Africa in 1955; these were all countries playing international cricket to different standards/levels at this time. The role of the EWCA in this demonstrates the centralised role that England played in the global game. It was decided that the first meeting would be in 1958 during the tour between England and Australia and at this time officers would be elected but between 1955 and 1958 it was decided that England would deal with the secretarial duties involved (Whitehorn, 1956). As an organisation, the EWCA was central in suggesting a global organisation and it was keen to control the development of the IWCC. After the constitution had been sent to other national governing bodies for discussion, the first meeting of the IWCC took place in Melbourne on 19 February 1958.

This meeting coincided with an England tour. Delegates from Australia, New Zealand, South Africa and England attended and Holland was represented (Heyhoe Flint and Rheinberg, 1976). At the meeting, a message from Vera Cox, President of the EWCA, was read:

> I should like to say to you at this exciting moment, when cricket delegates of many countries are gathered together "may good counsel and wisdom attend your deliberations for the encouragement of women cricketers all over the world". I have a vision of tours and Test Matches in all continents in the not too distant future, resulting in mutual understanding and lasting friendship. (cited in Heyhoe Flint and Rheinberg, 1976: 54)

There is no record of any statements being read by other presidents of national governing bodies; this might reflect the position of the EWCA in terms of its role in the development of the organisation, again illustrating the central role of the EWCA in the formation of the IWCC. The power of the EWCA in the IWCC continues in the initial history of the organisation.

The formation of the IWCC allowed for some consensus to be developed on issues such as the 'laws of the game', which followed the laws of men's cricket. No adaptations were made to these apart from the endorsement of the 5-oz ball, which is slightly smaller than the ball used in international men's cricket. This was decided as it was already the case in the national governing body rules and the smaller ball was thought to suit women's smaller hand and it is still the case today that women play with the 5.0-oz ball. Test matches were decided to be played over three days. The decision to adapt to the men's game without any modification is interesting, as this does signify a difference compared to other women's sport, in which modifications often were encouraged to suit women's perceived fragility. This might be explained by the separate governance of men's and women's cricket, which adopted the format of men's cricket without any pressure to modify the game, as there is little evidence of any communication between the IWCC and ICC. Being a separate organisation enabled the game to develop in specific ways aligned with the men's game, which was accepted by the women as the established form of the game.

It is not known whether the ICC was aware of the formation of the IWCC, but it is unlikely that they took any notice of the organisation in the early days. On the contrary, the outsider group was far more aware of the established group, and in adopting the men's game and the rules that were established by them, a desire to mimic the game is evident, in an attempt to be a legitimate group that played cricket according to the established traditions of the game. This desire to mimic aspects of the established group is not unusual in established and outsider figurations, as a common characteristic of the outsider group is that the outsider group often pays more attention to the established group than vice versa. Women cricketers were acutely aware of the ICC's governance of the men's game (and the MCC's role in this), but there is little evidence or awareness of the ICC regarding the women's game. The power balances between the two groups were so extensive that the established group and the outsider group could coexist in harmonious inequality and had no need to be interdependent on one another; the established group had clear monopolisation of key resources, rules of the game, finances and facilities, whilst women were dependent on the men's game for the laws of the game. At the time of the formation of the IWCC, extensive power imbalances in the established and outsider figuration existed and the outsider group did not appear to challenge this or contact the established group. At the first meeting, the purposes/aims of the IWCC were defined as being to

- Further cricket among women and girls at an international level
- Promote international tours
- Provide a liaison between tours
- Legislate on any problems which could not be resolved mutually (Women's Cricket History, 2012–2015).

The president and secretary who were elected were from the EWCA and the vice president was elected from South Africa. Again the EWCA had a strong presence in the committee, perhaps reflecting the EWCA's involvement but also the reliance of other countries on the EWCA for the development of the organisation. At the first meeting, a discussion about tour schedule emerged; however, from the outset, the organisation was beset with the issue of finances and the discussion of a tour schedule illustrates the difficulties facing the women's game, as without the finances to support the development of such a schedule, national governing bodies could not commit to a schedule; so a provisional schedule emerged. Mirroring the problems at a national level, the IWCC had similar financial issues and it was evident from the outset that financing a global organisation was going to be challenging; whilst the purpose of the IWCC was clearly defined, the resources to achieve this were less evident. A discussion about finances agreed that each council was allowed two delegates, member associations with more than 20 clubs affiliated were to pay £2 and those with fewer than 20 clubs were charged 15 shillings (sterling in both cases). The fact that an association could join with less than 20 clubs demonstrated that the women's game was not playing extensively at this time.

The next meeting was held on 28 December 1960 in Durban, during a tour between England and South Africa. All countries had delegates present other than Australia and New Zealand. It was noted that cricket was being played in Canada and Ireland and that the organisation was hopeful that these countries might join. Two officers from Australia and one from Holland were elected. Discussions about the format of test match cricket and about changing the number of balls bowled in an over were rejected. Changes to a tour schedule were needed to ensure that countries could finance the tours. Three years later, on 4 July 1963, the third meeting was held in England during the Australia–England series. At the outset and in these early days, the role of the IWCC was still quite uncertain. This is in stark contrast to the ICC, which from the beginning had been exclusionary in its categorisation of who could be members and had clear categories in relation to test match cricket and membership criteria. However, the IWCC did not have the ability to be selective; as the outsider group, its desire to develop the game ensured a more inclusive governing body. At the 1963 meeting, finances were discussed again, an ongoing issue.

The problem facing national governing bodies was lack of funds, and this is mirrored in the development of the IWCC. At the 1963 meeting, it was decided that tours should not take place more than every four years to allow time for fundraising and financial planning. Without a clear financial plan and due to the sporadic timing of meetings, the IWCC seemed to lack power in the governance of the game. Instead the key nations seemed to influence the game more in line with national agendas, and a consequence of this was that the IWCC did not develop strong governance of the game. One of the key issues was that those involved in running the IWCC voluntarily often had voluntary positions in their own national organisations as well as having full-time jobs; thus the organisations were stretched in having people who could dedicate themselves to the development of the organisations.

As an organisation, the IWCC had difficulties in maintaining organisational responsibilities, and at the next meeting in London on 4 August 1966, in conjunction with the New Zealand tour of England, no members were nominated for vice president and so none were elected. This demonstrates an issue in the governance of the organisation in which time for such a position was lacking amongst members. In the end, a member from Australia was elected. Lack of funding was discussed again, but there seemed to be little impetus to be able to solve the issue of funding; all positions in the IWCC were voluntary and there was no discussion in any of the official minutes about possibilities of support from the ICC. The struggles of the IWCC are captured in the IWCC minutes of the 1966 meeting: 'It was felt that, as the national administrators were already over-burdened, the appointment of a permanent Liaison Officer by them might ease the burden' (Women's Cricket History, IWCC, 4th meeting). At this meeting, the tour schedule was once again amended due to tours being cancelled.

There are no records of discussion about the ICC and men's cricket, although at this time, through the records of the EWCA there was awareness of the men's game and vice versa, but in the minutes of the IWCC, these discussions are absent, and at no point from 1956 to 1966 is there any discussion about links with the ICC. At the 1969 meeting on 19 February in New Zealand, Jamaica affiliated to the IWCC. This was the first time since the emergence of the organisation in 1958 that a new country affiliated, perhaps illustrating the slow growth of the women's game during this time period (at least in relation to international competition). Jamaica quickly played a role in the international game and its member became the IWCC vice president, perhaps illustrating the inclusivity of the IWCC which was keen to involve new organisations and new people in the development of the IWCC. Representation of all countries and delegates at meetings was proving challenging for the organisation, as the minutes outline:

Due to several delegates being unable to attend the entire meeting, a representative discussion could not take place on the provisional Tour Schedule. It was agreed the Hon. Secretary should liaise with the Committee of the New Zealand Council and utilise the services of a computer to program a new Schedule.

Also discussed at the meeting was the issue of amateur status. This is interesting as all female cricketers were amateur (by virtue of the game not being financed) not necessarily because there was any objection to professionalism, although there was likely to be a range of views on the issues of being paid to play cricket, as there continued to be issues relating to these broader issues in the men's game.

At the 6th meeting on 2 August 1973 in London, India and Trinidad and Tobago attended but were not fully admitted; again their attendance shows a growth in the women's game from the initial countries involved. Interestingly at this meeting it was decided that all the officers would come from England and so three officers were elected. This might represent a desire for the founding nations to retain control of the game as more countries joined or started to show an interest in international cricket. A discussion ensued about the Caribbean countries playing as the West Indies as they do in men's international competition, and this was agreed. The World Cup was discussed, but this was being organised by the hosting country, England, as the IWCC did not have sufficient governance to be the organiser of the event. A discussion about qualification for playing for a national side was agreed, and it was agreed that three years of residence would be suitable. At the following meeting held in London on 9 August 1976, it was decided to reelect the same officers. During this meeting, it was decided that a code of conduct relating to sponsorship was required. India quickly started to have influence in the IWCC, as after South Africa was deemed unable to host the 1978 World Cup, India offered and was accepted as the host country. At the 8th meeting of the IWCC held in India on 11 January 1978, the minutes indicated the lack of control that the IWCC had in overseeing the arrangements of a global tournament, despite being the global governing body:

> Concern was expressed at the lack of direction given by the Council regarding the World Cup arrangements and it was agreed that the IWCC should become pro-active regarding future venues and arrangements. (Women's Cricket History, 2012–2014)

The host national governing body had more control over the organisation of the tournament than the IWCC, and this was something discussed at the IWCC, but again there seems to be little resolution to this situation. During this time, a key development in the women's game evolved as the first World Cup for either men or women was played. The discussion about the emergence of the World Cup had started in 1971. Jack Hayward, a businessman already involved in funding Jamaican cricket, had offered to fund the event. At the 1971 annual general meeting (AGM), the EWCA agreed for the first World Cup to go ahead. Again the role of the EWCA in this suggests that the national governing bodies had more influence in the development of the international game than the IWCC. At this time, South Africa had not been invited to play as a country but as individual players to make up an International XI; but this had to be reconsidered and finally no South African players were involved. Seven teams that reflected the make-up of the IWCC at the time–England, Young England, Australia, Jamaica, New Zealand, Trinidad and Tobago, and an International XI–competed in a series of 60-over one-day matches, each team playing the rest. Australia and England played the final at Edgbaston; England won and the team members were handed a trophy by Princess Anne. The tournament structure was later copied by the ICC, with the men's World Cup being played in England in 1975. At this time in the men's game, test cricket was still the most dominant prestigious form, so the introduction of the one-day World Cup format was interesting and, for some, controversial. Yet, for women's cricket, one-day internationals were already widely played and accepted, mainly due to lack of time and access to facilities which suited one-day cricket; so the women's teams were less dogmatic about the forms of cricket being played and this may explain why the World Cup format was accepted so willingly in the women's game.

The 9th meeting of the IWCC was held in Christchurch, New Zealand, on 5 February 1982. All the elected posts were taken by Australia; from 1958 to 1982, most of these posts had been held by the founding nations, but with the dominance of England and Australia. At this meeting, sponsorship of the game was discussed at length, and it was recognised that sponsorship was going to be an essential part of the global women's game, although little detail is evident about what sponsorship was evident and how this differed in the different countries affiliated to the IWCC. Membership fees were increased again.

At the 10th meeting held on 22 January 1985 in Melbourne, Denmark and Ireland joined the IWCC. Current officers of Australia remained in post and thus the dominance of the founding nations in positions of authority in the IWCC continued, and this may reflect a desire to ensure control over the global governance of the game. These founding nations fully understood the complexity of increasing affiliation and the challenges it may bring in terms of control over the development of the women's game. Denmark and Ireland joining the IWCC illustrates the differing trajectory of the men's and women's game, as neither of these countries has ever been a full member of the ICC. During this meeting, a discussion about membership categories was raised but this was in relation to whether men could act as delegates (Women Cricket Associates, 2012). Prior to this decision, men had not been able to act as delegates. The reason for this is unclear, but it illustrates the strictly (whether intentional or not) women-only policy of the IWCC up to this point. Other decisions made at the meeting centred on the IWCC and it needing a logo to represent and reflect the global game. The fact that the organisation had existed for so long without such representation demonstrates how the organisation existed but that governance remained weak.

At the 11th meeting in London on 26 July 1987, finances of the tour were discussed. World Cup rules were debated and rules regarding playing in World Cup were adopted. This is the first time in the history of the IWCC that the organisation played a role in the governance of the global game and decided on global rules governing international competition. Issues of sponsorship were discussed alongside ongoing concerns about the identity of the IWCC. Discussions about World Cup payments and the amateur status of women's cricket were raised but not resolved.

The 12th meeting was held in Australia on 15 December 1988 and the minutes show lengthy discussions about the IWCC, including issues such as improving communication between the IWCC and its members. The need to attract international sponsorship to aid future tournaments is discussed but this is not resolved, and it appears that continual issues about finance impact on the organisation.

In 1990, a meeting was held in the northern hemisphere and a European Cup was decided on, to be started in 1995 and to be played every two years. The European Cup was considered a useful way to have more regular international competition between the countries in close proximity to one another, that is, Ireland, Holland and England, which were all playing cricket at this time. The meetings held by the IWCC continue to be sporadic, but at the 13th meeting of the organisation, Pakistan attended the meeting, although it did not apply for membership. At this meeting, it was decided that the IWCC would be the governing body for the World Cup, European Cup and Shell Rose Bowl. The fact that the organisation had not been the controlling body for these international competitions once again underlines the difficulties that the organisation had in governing or controlling the development of the global game; instead a number of players at national levels were controlling its development, the nations of England and Australia in particular.

At the 14th meeting in Auckland, it is stated that membership queries had been received from Canada, Japan and Sweden. Canada and Japan were accepted as affiliate members of the IWCC, but what this means in relation to their involvement is unclear; also it is unclear how much cricket was played in these countries. By 1997, the organisation was in severe financial decline, and a one-off levy was raised on all members. Pakistan and Sri Lanka were admitted as members in 1997; thus, by 1997, nine member organisations were represented. In the minutes of the 1997 meeting, the ICC is mentioned for the first time in discussions, and this too is only in brief when it is noted that a draft strategic plan and budget for the next five years was presented to the ICC. It is unclear whether this was requested by the ICC or what prompted this presentation of plans, but it is the first time that the ICC was mentioned in any official records of the IWCC, and may signal the first discussions that began to identify greater interdependency between the two organisations. Running parallel to the development of the IWCC is the Women's World Cup and this is discussed briefly below before drawing out some issues relating to the development of the IWCC.

Women's World Cup and the IWCC

The development of the World Cup as an international tournament also illustrates some key trends that run parallel in understanding the global development of women's cricket. The first World Cup was funded by a West Indian businessman. It was organised and hosted in England (again not surprising given the dominance of England more broadly). The second World Cup was held in India in 1977/78 and was won by Australia. In this event, only four countries participated – England, Australia, India and New Zealand. The West Indies, who had been due to participate, had to withdraw at the last minute due to funding issues and internal disputes. With only four countries participating, this was a disappointing World Cup as it did not show any development in the international game since 1973. In fact the number of countries participating declined during this period. The tournament was held in India amidst difficulties in terms of another country being able to host the World Cup due to lack of funds and support. In 1982 New Zealand hosted the World Cup; the West Indies once again did not play and only four countries played, and Australia won again. The sporadic nature of the World Cup shows the issues facing the global development of women's cricket; without solid funding or governance, tour schedules and international competition schedules continued to prove challenging.

At the 1988 World Cup, which was played in Australia, the number of participating countries increased, with Holland, India, Ireland and the West Indies joining New Zealand, Australia and England. Australia won again, illustrating their playing dominance in the international game. The fifth World Cup, in 1993, was once again hosted in England with Australia, Denmark, Holland, India, Ireland, New Zealand and the West Indies playing. The final was played at Lord's on 1 August (the first match to be played at Lord's); England beat New Zealand in the final. The sixth World Cup in 1997 saw a further increase in the number of participants, with Pakistan, South Africa and Sri Lanka playing for the first time. Australia beat New Zealand to win the World Cup. The seventh World Cup under the auspices of the IWCC was played in New Zealand and was won by New Zealand for the first time. By this time, in 2000, a draft strategic plan and budget had already been presented to the ICC. This set the path for the merger of the IWCC and the ICC in 2005, which appears to have been prompted by further financial issues and in particular the potential collapse of the World Cup in South Africa in 2005 due to lack of funds. Australia once again won the World Cup in 2005. Australia's dominance throughout the World Cup history, with England and New Zealand also featuring, demonstrates the lack of competitive cricket played internationally.

The history of the IWCC and the emergence of the World Cup demonstrate long-term social processes which can identify a trajectory of development. The emergence of the IWCC as a global organisation is significant and demarcates where women's cricket was played and which countries were instrumental in the development of a global women's game. However, the IWCC and the problems it faced illustrate broader power relations and the outsider position of women's cricket in the global cricket figuration in which women's cricket remains separate, distinct and lacking in governance. The IWCC is not an organisation that can afford to have headquarters or a paid committee that steers its development; it is in effect an extension of the national governing bodies' officers. In particular, there is a trend in which Australia and England seem to dominate within the positions of power in the organisation, as they do more broadly in international competitions such as the World Cup where they are dominant in winning international tournaments. The IWCC is willing to allow other countries to join and does not seem to have regulations about the playing status of the countries joining. Australia and England enable countries to join but continue to shape the development of the international game by ensuring that they are in control of the key positions within the organisation, but also a lack of wider growth becomes problematic for the women's game. The women's game remains amateur with little income sources from either sponsorship or commercial developments in the game, reliant on benevolent individuals. As cricket in the main ICC nations is monopolised by the men's game, people pay to watch the national team, bringing with it feelings of pride, which is supported by the media and the emergence of national heroes; but for the women's game success does not bring money or status and thus funds were not available for the IWCC or national governing bodies.

The merger of the IWCC and the ICC

The merger between the IWCC and the ICC, which seems to have been prompted predominantly due to financial issues, begins a significant trend in the development of women's cricket globally. The media reports at the time of the merger are telling, as the *BBC Sport* website reports, 'ICC Saves Women's World Cup' (Heinrich, 2004). South Africa is firmly considered to be at blame for the lack of organisation, as an IWCC report to the BBC says, 'They should have got their act together' (cited in Heinrich, 2004). The view that the ICC saved the IWCC sheds some insight into the role of the ICC and the IWCC in the mergers; it presents the ICC in a positive light, keen to support women's cricketers, at a time when issues of gender and equity in sport more broadly are becoming more prominent. In the media reports, an IWCC spokeswoman claims the ICC merger is because 'the IWCC simply doesn't have the resources, so the merger means the ICC can be more pro-active on women's cricket' (Heinrich, 2004). In the discussion of a merger, it is not considered that the ICC might further support the development of the IWCC or fund the World Cup but merging is considered the way forward.

The merger with the ICC created a subcommittee within the ICC; the women's cricket council became a subsection of the ICC and was responsible for the continual development of the game, in line with broader ICC strategies and developments. A Women's Cricket Advisory Group was formed, whose role is to make recommendations to the ICC Development Committee on all matters relating to women's cricket. With the merger, the IWCC became part of a more established organisation, one that has global governance and one that has monopoly of key resources, which in theory the women's game should be able to access. On the other hand, it also puts in a wider, much larger organisation that has other agendas and competing agendas that might run contrary to women's cricket or might fail to account for the development of women's cricket or prioritise this element of the game. Despite this, the IWCC had little choice in the merger; the history of the organisation shows the challenges it faced, and ultimately for the women's game to survive the merger had to take place, but this places the women's game in a much larger figuration, with more players, and ultimately their ability to control the outcome for women's cricket becomes far less possible.

Expansion of the women's game was relatively rapid after the ICC involvement; in 2009, the ICC Women's World Cup was played in Australia. Six teams automatically qualified, and these were Australia, New Zealand, England, Sri Lanka, India and the West Indies; this was decided after they finished within the top six in 2005. South Africa and Pakistan then qualified after a World Cup qualifier held in South Africa. This was the first time a qualifier had been played for the women's game. And by 2009, the ICC suggests that it had 59 member countries with girls' or women's cricket; this may highlight that more nations had women and girls playing that were not affiliated to the IWCC but may also be the result of the ICC mandate forcing more countries to develop the women's and girls' game. This mandate, which was developed after the merger of the IWCC and the ICC, insisted that all national governing bodies had to merge to create one governing body for men's and women's cricket. The mandate significantly impacted on the global development of women's cricket, and now women's cricket, in all the ICC full member countries (and a number of others in associate categories), is represented by one national governing body whose responsibility it is to develop women's cricket in line with broader national and international policies. These mergers represent a significant shift in power between men's and women's cricket in which interdependency between the two groups has increased.

Despite the ICC mandate requiring all national governing bodies to represent the men's and women's game, both Australia and England had merged with their male national governing bodies prior to the ICC mandate: England in 1998 and Australia in 2001. These mergers are significant in signalling a change in power relations between men's and women's cricket, which had prior to this largely been separate organisations that had coexisted but levels of interdependency between the men's and women's game has not been extensive. In the following section, I explore the preconditions that enabled the merger between men's and women's cricket associations to take place and consider how and why organisations merged with male national governing bodies. Specifically I consider how this can be explained in relation to other significant social processes, considering the power balances and how these power balances shift in such mergers and how women as a group have developed greater access to significant power resources to enable these mergers to take place.

Gender relations, power and gender integration in governing bodies

In England, the EWCA had struggled financially for some time as an amateur organisation; its members had relied on volunteers to enable a successful national governing body, although this became more and more challenging as the organisation developed. The financial problems that the organisation faced are evident through the year books, AGM meetings and notes (Velija et al., 2010). Numerous conversations and reports illustrate the difficulties the organisation had in funding the development of the women's game. As an outsider organisation that relied predominantly on volunteers, obtaining the funding required to continue was a constant challenge. In the 1980s and 1990s, funding became more and more problematic. This despite a successful World Cup win in 1993 (the team continued to be successful); with the women's game getting little finance, sponsorship, media coverage or strategic plan to develop, the EWCA had no source of funding. The women's game did not reflect national identity in the way that men's cricket did and men's cricket continued to be the dominant sport; the 1993 World Cup win by England was not really celebrated by the wider sporting community.

At the 1989 AGM, the severity of the financial situation resulted in a serious discussion about whether the organisation should continue. As an outsider group with limited interdependency between the established and the outsider groups, the women did not have access to resources, either financial or otherwise, to continue. The organisation was quite insular, and this may have been in part for fear of being seen as too radical and it did not want to challenge or insist on support. As an organisation, it was relatively self-sufficient apart from the finances and the need for support to access pitches. The EWCA approach was one of separatism, and hence it did not seek support from the England and Wales Cricket Board (ECB) nor expect it. This may have been for fear of criticism from the established group, or it may have been due to the nature of considering the EWCA as a separate organisation, run by women for women (as evidenced by the fact that men were not allowed to vote until 1993).

This is seen clearly in the organisation's approaches to using women in support roles, the only country to do so and this was particularly the case with umpires. Other countries were reliant on 'qualified men umpires', but in England this was not the case (Heyhoe Flint and Rheinberg, 1976: 155). There had always been an impetus in the EWCA to develop and support women umpires, and the top women umpires were recognised by the men's association of cricket umpires. The qualification for umpires is the same for men and women, which involves an examination and practical experience. Although men did umpire some women's matches, the test matches and ODIs were only umpired by women. It was not until 1996 that men were allowed to umpire, and this was after a relaxation of the rules and perhaps was in relation to the fact that two years later the EWCA merged with the ECB. Women umpires were not paid for umpiring at international matches and they did not even claim expenses, so those involved had to fund their own involvement in the game. With travel, accommodation and other expenses, such commitment could be expensive, suggesting that those who were involved had the funds to be able to support and sustain their umpire status.

Similar to women playing cricket and concerns about dress, there was also concern about women and their appearance whilst umpiring. Female umpires in England wore skirts, the reason being, as described by the EWCA, 'to avoid any look of masculinity' (Heyhoe Flint and Rheinberg, 1976: 157). The desire to avoid being masculine in this context says something more broadly about women's role in cricket and the wider issues of gender relations and perceptions about masculinity and femininity, which were largely accepted by the established and the outsider groups. Cricket was firmly established as a male sport and women interested in the game were tolerated and allowed to play; they did draw suspicion about their masculinity (and sexuality). To counter this, playing or umpiring in 'feminine ways' was essential to the EWCA, and this was most apparent in the dress codes that all members were expected to adhere to; articles about women's dress, length of shorts, skirts and socks, and how to iron clothing were regular in *Women's Cricket* magazine. Again this seems to have been in part the strategy of the EWCA to accept, and not challenge, the established male group, largely internalising the view that women's cricket was secondary to men's cricket. This reflects a form of 'harmonious' inequality and women largely accepted this secondary position because they did not have the power to challenge this position; but the women also accepted that the women's game was not the same as the men's game and were largely happy to accept this. As long as they could play cricket, they did not appear to expect support and they were acutely aware of the need to be seen to be grateful when accessing men's resources, and keen to be seen as polite and 'professional'. Code of conduct and behaviour were also frequent reports in *Women's Cricket* magazine. These reports are reflective of the monopolisation of the established group, which was able to not only monopolise resources (such as physical resources) but also monopolise the ideology of cricket as a male sport, a sport that is strongly linked to masculinity and nationality. Although women umpired women's matches and some lower-level men's matches, there is little evidence to indicate that women who were qualified to do so umpired at top levels of the men's game, probably as they were not asked to do so. Yet in relation to umpiring, the number of women who were qualified to umpire demonstrates a commitment on behalf of the EWCA to involve women at all levels of the game and was part of an unintended strategy to be self-sufficient.

By the 1990s, the EWCA was struggling to continue, and in 1997 in the magazine *Wicket Women*, a possible merger with the ECB was published. At this stage, it was explained that formal negotiations with the ECB should be viewed as an opportunity that they could not ignore:

> The fact is that if we stay as we are, we will not be able to meet growing demand. Considering a merger with the ECB is an opportunity to plan for and stimulate growth in women's cricket, it is opportunity we cannot afford to miss. (Daniels, cited in Harris, 1997)

The discussions about the merger continued and articles written by the Chairman and Chief Executive of the EWCA discussed the merger. To further support the merger, in 1998 the ECB and EWCA commissioned Inform Associates, a research company, to conduct a review of the position of women's cricket. The report concluded that 'the development of cricket for women and girls needs to be mainstreamed within cricket development', thus advocating the proposed merger and citing several reasons for how this could benefit women's cricket in England. The discussion about mainstreaming the women's game is something that has been discussed at length in relation to women's sport. Mainstreaming and merging of organisations has been discussed in relation to power and gender more broadly. One of the consequences of these mergers, as proposed by Morrison (1993), is that these mergers give women greater access to facilities, finances and coaching. On the other hand, women often lose out on administrative autonomy (Morrison, 1993); thus mergers represent both enabling and constraining opportunities for women in sport. Applying Elias' concepts of game models to these mergers may help to consider power and the relational aspect of power in such mergers.

Not all members of the EWCA were supportive of the merger with the ECB, demonstrating that within the EWCA there were differences of opinion in relation to the merger. In the period leading up to the vote, power struggles within the organisation became more apparent.

At the emergency general meeting (EGM) held on 29 March 1998, the organisation needed a two-thirds majority vote to enforce the proposed merger. The vote was close and 30 members abstained from voting to protest against the merger. The concerns about the proposed merger from those opposing it seemed to focus on (1) the concern that the benefit would only be at the elite level of the game at the expense of the grass roots, (2) the concern about the loss of identity of the women's game and (3) the concern that women would lose autonomy over the game more broadly. Despite these concerns, the vote was close but enough to agree to the merger; the merger went ahead and in 1998 the EWCA was dissolved and became a part of the ECB.

Those opposing the merger were concerned about power and control over the women's game and how this would affect their own roles. This is a fear amongst women that is not uncommon in other sport mergers (Shaw and Slack, 2002). In particular, the chief concern of some members of the EWCA was about whether the future development of the women's game would benefit by integrating with the ECB or, on the other hand, whether women cricketers and the women's game would continue to be peripheral to the men's game if it did not merge. Therefore, there was an air of resignation that the merger was inevitable, but the merger was not necessarily embraced by all of those involved in the WCA (1998). At the time of the merger, the EWCA (1986) insisted that the head of women's cricket should be a woman who has previously played for England. The members felt that this would ensure that a woman at least holds a senior management position within the ECB to ensure the women's game was not forgotten. This insistence was made by the EWCA as part of the merger, as it was aware that the position of women was likely to change.

In the Australian context, a similar picture can be identified. Financial issues in the Australian Women's Cricket Council (AWCC) are also frequently discussed throughout the history of the organisation, and in 1996 and 2000, these financial issues were of concern to the organisation. Like in England, it was not entirely clear whether the game could continue (Stronach and Adair, 2009). Funding, coaching, sponsorship and development were frequently highlighted as problems. Australia, like England, had been successful and largely dominant in relation to their success; it had won the Ashes from 1984 to 2002 and had won five out of the seven World

Cup competitions. Despite this success, the team struggled to develop financially sustainable options, largely the result of being the outsider group in an established and outsider figuration and not having the ability to influence financial developments. Like in England, the Australian women's game did not reflect feelings of national identity that would have evoked support for women's cricket, and the game remained in relation to men's cricket relatively invisible, with few people aware of the success of the team. Like the EWCA, the AWCC was dependent on volunteers, with only two full-time members of staff. As a result of these continuing difficulties, the AWCC integrated with the Australian Cricket Board (ACB) in 2001, and after two years the organisation changed its name to Cricket Australia to reflect this broader change and integrated organisation.

In both England and Australia, it is unclear as to whether without the financial difficulties either organisation would have chosen to merge. Both organisations were 'forced' in many respects to merge, because for the women's game to continue they had to find a way to fund the game and the only way to do so was to merge with the respective male organisations. Yet this was not wholly supported by those within the respective organisations; one trend emerges in exploring both case studies and that is that both organisations went into their mergers as the weaker organisation (Stronach and Adair, 2009). Inwardly both organisations discussed at length the merger and had concerns about the proposals; however these concerns were not raised outwardly as the EWCA and the AWCC were keen to be seen as cooperative and supportive of the merger, presumably for fear that the merger may not take place and that may leave the organisations financially unable to continue. Indicative of the power balances between the two groups, the male organisations are relatively silent about the mergers. Why do male organisations 'bail' women out in this particularly context at this time? Given the history of the two organisations and the fact that the women's game remained separate for so long, this is an important question to ask here. Sociologically, it is not useful to see the male organisations as benevolent providers of the women's game or as malicious in trying to take over and control the women's game, but instead it is useful to consider what are the social processes that led to the mergers described above, both nationally and internationally/globally. Critically the question is how might we explain the integration of male and female sporting organisations at this specific time in relation to wider social processes and gender relations at this time? In the following section I explore the relationship between functional democratization and wider policies of gender relations.

Functional democratisation, gender relations and the mergers between the EWCA and the ECB and between the AWCC and the ACB

In discussing gender relations a figurational analysis considers the monopoly of physicality (violence), ideologies (knowledge) and organisational networks (interdependence) as being central to an analysis of social life and gender relations more broadly (Mierzwinski et al., 2014). In considering women's cricket and its development, these factors form a useful analysis for explaining the development of the women's game. At the heart of these are broader questions about power relations and how one group continues over time to monopolise key resources that enable established and outsider relations to continue.

Functional democratisation is a term to describe shifting power relations and is central in understanding a figurational approach to power and interdependence (Dunning and Hughes, 2013). In particular, Elias highlights industrialisation, economic growth, urbanisation and bureaucratisation as social processes that influence social structures and social transformation of power. These processes include the 'emergence of larger more differentiated and denser chains of interdependence' (Dunning and Hughes, 2013: 67). Thus through specialisation of roles, Elias demonstrates how power is likely to become more equal. Outsider groups are more likely to be successful in challenging power if they are able to organise themselves and disrupt wider chains of interdependence, and over time, denser chains of interdependency create more reciprocal dependency, and these processes are critical in understanding how groups have more control. It is important to note that processes of equalisation do not result in equality, and inequalities still exist, but crucially reciprocal dependency enables the outsider group to have a power resource which may enable power imbalances to become more equalised.

Through tracing the development of women's cricket over a significant time period, it is evident that there have been long-term social processes that have lessened power imbalances between the two groups. This represents a trend towards equalisation as can be seen in the development of the game globally, and the merger between men's and women's organisations is further evidence of greater levels of interdependency. At the time of the merger in both Australia and England, and at the time of the merger between the IWCC and the ICC, it was not deemed appropriate for men's organisations to let women's cricket just dissolve, and as discussed elsewhere in the English context, it was perceived that no responsible governing body could allow that to happen (Malcolm and Velija, 2008). What social processes had influenced the position of women's cricket to allow the game to have increased power resource to allow such mergers to occur? Why did the ECB accept the merger? Why did the ICC and the IWCC merge? I propose two significant social processes that influenced these mergers. The first is the emergence of equity policies and increase in 'equality policies in sport more broadly' and how some attitudes to female sports had become more intolerable and thresholds of repugnance and inequity had shifted. This is evidenced in the moral and media backlash against the MCC when it decided not to allow women to become members of the MCC. This incidence highlights a shift in power in cricket, in relation to gender and class, as well as highlighting the differing attitudes of the established and outsider groups to continual exclusion from the MCC. In considering the merger of the IWCC and the ICC in 2005, it is important to draw on wider social processes and the increase in global women's movements and policies to address inequities of gender that have enabled a shift in gender relations more broadly and are tied into 'moral' arguments about the worth of women's sport; this in itself has become a power resource for women's rights.

Gender equity, the state and gender relations in sport

As argued in Chapter 1, the introduction of the welfare state and increase in women's rights more broadly, that is, reproductive rights, protection against male violence and education for women, all demonstrate a civilising direction in respect of women's rights more broadly (Dunning, 1999). In sport, state intervention in leisure and sports is of importance in trying to locate the broader development of women's cricket in long-term social processes. The role of the state in the delivery (funding) of sport is critical in thinking about equity policies and sport-for-all policies more broadly. In considering first the merger between the EWCA and the ECB, it is critical to understand the role of the nation state and changing legalisation which influenced changes in organisational networks. The Sports Council (formed in 1972), now Sport England, was instrumental in making decisions about funding sports; at the outset, the Sports Council had an initial ethos of encouraging sport for all.

Legislation plays a part in reducing the monopolisation of men in certain sports, as organisational networks previously resistant to change can recognise and, to a certain extent, fund women's sport. This is linked more broadly to the social processes around the politicisation of sport and sport policies in the UK. In the UK, the Sports Council was also instrumental in trying to address financial discrimination against women's sport. One of the key changes in this approach was that in 1987, it was made obligatory for organisations that received Sport Council grants to provide equal opportunities for men and women, through strategy, strategic planning and policies. This is expected to be monitored through the organisation's approach to equity. This signals a significant shift in women's sport as such a policy provides a power resource (albeit a small one). To receive funding, organisations must at least start to recognise the needs of minority groups in sport and start to commit on paper and policy a redistribution of resources to consider women's involvement in sport.

Equity policies are also seen in global processes in sport, for example, the emergence of the International Association of Physical Education and Sport for Girls and Women (IAPESGW), formed in 1949 in the USA, and the International Working Group on Women and Sport (IWG), founded in the UK in 1994 after the Brighton Declaration on Sport. This reflects several examples of coalition (and global social processes) in which the outsider group has collectively organised itself to challenge the ideologies (knowledge) that have enabled men to monopolise key resources in sport by challenging dominant ideologies and organisational networks that prevent women's access to sport. The international women and sport movement from 1994 was instrumental in outlining an international strategy for developing women's sport and the Brighton Declaration on Women and Sport provides an opportunity for government and non-government organisations to commit (at least on paper) to a strategy for the development of women's sport. The Brighton Declaration was developed from a conference held in Brighton, UK, jointly by the Sports Council and the International Olympic Committee (IOC). The purpose of the declaration was as follows:

> The Declaration is addressed to all governments, public authorities, organisations, businesses, educational and research establishments, women's organisations and individuals who are responsible for, or who directly or indirectly influence, the conduct, development or promotion of sport or who are in any way involved in the employment, education, management, training, development or care of women in sport. (UK Sports Council, 1994: 3)

The ongoing work of the IWG and the conferences held on women and sport have enabled key changes in the profile of women's sport in global sporting organisations, for example, the IOC. These organisations raise the profile of women's rights and also include discussions about women and sport through the United Nations and Sport Development projects.

Gender relations in cricket: Gender equity and the MCC

At the time of the merger between the EWCA and the ECB in 1998, a significant issue in relation to gender and functional democratisation more broadly can be seen, when the MCC, the most established male preserve in cricket, voted to allow female members. The MCC was no longer the governing body for English cricket nor did it have the role it used to have in the global game; nevertheless, the ideological position of the MCC as the home of English cricket is significant. At the initial vote 'a secret ballot showed 55.7% of members favour letting in women. But 66% was needed to scrap the 211-year-old ban' (*The Sun*, 25 February 1998). Despite this being a secret vote, media publicity was extensive and this signals a shift from 1991 when only 38% of members voted to allow female members. The MCC has been a male-only establishment since its formation and it had continued to insist on remaining a male-only organisation, despite being aware of the women's game and women cricketers. There was extensive media coverage of the decision of the MCC and some critique of the MCC in media reports on the issue. The criticism levelled at the MCC is however just as much levelled at the elitism and class-related issues as it is about gender relations. However, the case of the MCC demonstrates two key issues. Firstly, there is a civilising direction in relation to women's cricket and gender relations in cricket more broadly (to suggest a vote should take place and also the fact that the reports about this and the MCC were negative). Secondly, the vote by the MCC also illustrates the continuing issues relating to women's cricket as it signals how men are able to monopolise resources and knowledge about women's involvement in the game. The use of the vote to decide whether women should be allowed into the MCC was happening at the same time that the merger of the EWCA and the ECB was occurring (also decided by vote). Six months after the first vote, after continued pressure on the MCC, in September 1998 the MCC voted again and the decision was to let women members join. Despite allowing female memberships at this vote, 4,072 members still voted against the motion (*The Sun*, 29 September 1998). Behind the momentum to allow female membership is enabling the MCC, one of the most established and arguably profitable sports organisations, to be eligible for lottery grants. The fact that so many members were still against female memberships and also that the female members would have to wait to join was discussed in several media reports;

> Despite the decision, women will have to join an 18-year waiting list with thousands of men. The MCC bar will also remain men-only. But MCC president Colin Ingleby-Mackenzie said: "It's fantastic news. We shouldn't be afraid of women, they're rather a nice species" (*The Sun*, 29 September 1998)

The decision was not wholly supported, with some members quitting in protest. The insistence of the male-only bar staying as a male-only bar highlights, as Dunning (1999) illustrates, for some men the desire to retain gender relations as an important part of their male identity in which male-only spaces are needed to ensure that this identity is retained. There is also the need to rely on wilful nostalgia in relation to reinventing the idea that cricket is and has always been a male sport. Inviting women to join the MCC diminishes the notion that cricket is a male sport, one that involves a type of male bonding and identity which some groups wish to continue, romanticising about the past in which gender relations were more unequal and a desire to retain these relations amidst much broader and wider changes in gender relations. In such private clubs, the 'we' identity of members is based on a strong identification on a shared identity that may be invented. Women represent a 'they' identity, which threatens the shared identity of the group that some members want to protect, mainly because the 'we' identity reflects a type of privilege and prestige and forms of power which are beneficial to those involved. Within this established group, there are those who wish to retain old traditions but also those who are willing to accept new members, demonstrating a fragmentation in the established group's views about outsider groups.

Policies such as those discussed above and lottery funding grants which insist on organisations demonstrating gender equity as part of the criteria for application can be critiqued extensively, but they do reflect a willingness of the state to intervene to legislate for equity, although the impact of these can be slow to see. For example, such a criterion can be crudely applied or promised in the documentation for grants, but much slower to implement. By 2008, ten years after changes to the membership category, only 62 out of 18,000 members were women (*The Independent*, 22 July 2008). Thus organisational networks may become more inclusive to women, but in reality access remains challenging.

Such legislative changes then are sometimes subject to extensive critique, yet the insistence on gender equity in sporting organisations to be able to access grants does signal a shift in power relations. Through taking a long-term approach to locating these changes, it is evident that women have access to power resources that increase the established group's dependency on the outsiders. It also gives the outsiders a platform to be able to critique the established group, through demonstrating that the promises made in policy documents are not being kept. As the established group becomes interdependent with the outsider group, it becomes more dependent and thus the power ratio moves in a more equalising direction. Although such processes take time, power ratios may equalise slowly (and are not necessarily always in one direction). Another consequence of greater interdependence between established and outsider groups is greater mutual identification and how new conduct and behaviour is expected from the established and outsider groups. This new standard of behaviour includes greater cooperation, and in the context of the established group, the group has to take more consideration of the outsider group; for example, it can no longer ignore the outsider group but has to demonstrate a level of support that is expected in relation to policy but also in relation to paying more attention to the outsider group. Of course such relations impact on both the established and the outsider groups and the outsider group can become more dependent on the established group to access key resources and these new relations continue to impact on the social identities of those involved. The outsider group could continue to request, through legalisation greater involvement; the established group may ignore many of these requests but may have to at least consider the needs of the outsider group.

The social function of a group for another group becomes a source of power (Van Stolk and Wouters, 1987). Moral arguments are used by groups to signal that women's sport and women should be included. Thus in the discussion about the MCC, the EWCA and the ECB, and the merger of the IWCC and ICC, moral arguments are used as a further source of power for women in cricket, as in relations of increased interdependence and where there is strong mutual identification between groups, there is 'high level of *mutual expected self-restraint*' (Van Stolk and Wouters, 1987: 84).

As seen in Chapters 2 and 3, female cricketers have been keen throughout history and in their established and outsider relations not to critique the male establishment; instead as is often found in such relations, they are more likely to identify with the established group. This continues to be the case (although in Chapter 5, I explore some ways in which women begin to question the outsider group), but at least publicly, and in relation to membership to the MCC, Heyhoe Flint, a high-profile former female cricketer, is keen to support the established organisation (that she is now a member of):

> The former England cricket captain Rachael Heyhoe Flint – one of the few women with honorary life membership – believes that fast-tracking women to redress the balance would be divisive. "Having waited 211 years to acquire membership, that's the one thing I stressed throughout the nine-year campaign: we didn't want any favours. The process of becoming a member is exactly the same as for the men, and why shouldn't it be?" (*The Independent*, 22 July 2008)

These patterns of behavioural ideals are difficult for some groups to challenge, as in women's cricket these patterns enabled women to play sport. Not challenging the established group was effective for female cricketers to play the game, and thus changing these behavioural ideals can be challenging for outsider groups who internalise these ideals. Heyhoe Flint's comments here do not seem that different from those made in *Women's Cricket* magazine in 1963, in which female cricketers when discussing the lack of media coverage state that 'none of us would deny we cannot hit a ball as hard as a man or bowl as fast, but our technique is probably as good' (Picton, cited in *Women's Cricket*, 1963: 23). This demonstrates the social habituses of various groups and the extent to which the outsider group is often attached to the established group and that such internalisation and acceptance of the social habituses of the established and outsider groups requires long-term social processes to change attitudes. It is difficult for outsider groups to begin to detach themselves from old patterns (Van Stolk and Wouters, 1987). This is illustrated in other figurational studies of gender relations; for example, Treibel (2001), who draws on Elias's game models to emphasise the dynamic and processual character of gender relations, concurs with Brinkgreve's argument that social relations which are moving towards equalisation are those most prone to conflict and questioning from both groups. As the mutual balance of power moves towards equalisation, some groups are keen to maintain their current position and monopoly of resources. Similarly both suggest that while 'figurational ideals of the gender, especially those of women, have changed . . . the figurational patterns have not changed very much . . . attitudes have changed but behaviour less so' (Treibel, 2001: 188).

The roles of both the state in legislating sport and global processes that emphasise broader social issues such as human rights are central to understanding the context of the merging of male and female cricket organisations (both nationally) and globally. Global politics continue to emphasise gender relations, and as part of both national governing bodies and global organisations, long-term processes indicate a mutual balance of power that is in flux and a shift in power relations which emphasises the importance of gender equity. Thus policies of equity and equality have global priority and have to a certain extent been seen as a reflection of a country's civilising direction more broadly, whereby issues of equity have been viewed increasingly as examples of levels of civilisation.

Concluding thoughts

Thus the mergers between the EWCA and the ECB, the AWCC and the ACB, and ultimately the IWCC and the ICC cannot be seen as occurring in isolation from wider social process of functional democratisation in relation to gender relations in specific societies, but these occurred through global processes and global organisations/ movements such as human rights. All however suggest a civilising direction in terms of gender relations and women's sport. They also suggest a trend towards equalisation and a reduction of power imbalances. These mergers between organisations took place at a specific time in which women had wider access to social relations more broadly and long-term social processes suggest a civilising direction in this regard.

In applying aspects of figurational sociology to understanding the development of an international governing body and the merging of men and women's sporting organisations, it is useful to note how Elias argued that emotions such as 'shame, embarrassment and indeed disgust or repugnance characterize a driving affective mechanism of social control' (Mansfield, 2010: 95). Elias defined shame as 'a fear of social degradation or, more generally, of other people's gestures of superiority' (Elias, 2000: 414–415), while embarrassment refers to the anxiety or discomfort one experiences at (perceived) breaches in social norms. A marker of 'more civilised bodies' is their greater self-regulation by these emotional responses. People involved in organisations such as the MCC, the ICC, the ECB and Cricket Australia can be encouraged to introduce women members through legalisation and policy that tie funding to equity; however this only relates to organisational networks, in terms of the social habituses of established and outsider groups. Groups, nations or organisations can be shamed into being perceived to have outdated views of gender relations. This may be a process required in ensuring that all full members of the ICC begin to support women's cricket. Such dual processes allow the outsider group access to power to challenge (albeit in small ways) power resources within the established and outsider figuration, moving towards equalisation.

These social relations undergoing processes of emancipation between established and outsider groups, as Brinkgreve (2004) has argued elsewhere, are no less problematic than previous relations.

On the contrary, Brinkgreve (2004) argues that such relations are most prone to conflict. Given this as men's and women's cricket both have become more interdependent and dependency ties have become denser; mutual power balances between them have decreased. The ICC, the ECB and the ACB merged with their female counterparts, in part because of a moral argument to support women cricketers and in part because of the wider context and legislative changes in policy and funding opportunities, which give women greater access to challenge existing structures and access key resources. These changes also occur in relation to psychogenesis, and changes in attitudes to women cricketers (by some of the established) reflect long-term processes which suggest a civilising direction and a reduction of power balances between men's and women's sport. That is not to say that relations have equalised, and there continue to be inequalities in the delivery of cricket and in the social habituses and identities of those involved in the game, which will be explored in the next chapter.

5
Cricket and Gendered National Identities: The Experiences of Women Who Play and Organise the 'Global Game'

In the majority of countries discussed in Chapter 3, it was evident that cricket was diffused at a time when it strongly reflected types of nationalism and masculinity. Wherever cricket was played in the ICC full member countries, it was played first and foremost as a male sport that reflected particular views of masculinity. Cricket also embodied a type of nationalism, firstly English nationalism, but in many later contexts cricket was shaped and developed in ways that reflected the national character of where it was played. The exception in this case is clearly in Ireland and Holland where varying patterns of diffusion can be seen and the game was different for men's and women's cricket in these case studies. This is a reminder as Malcolm (2013) highlights that diffusion processes are not linear and there is no clear pattern of diffusion and acceptance of a sport; instead there are complex social processes that influence the acceptance or rejection of particular sport forms. However, it is important to consider in relation to gender the way cricket came to embody particular types of national identity and character. National identities related to nationalism are fluid and subject to change. The majority of research on sport and national identity is written about men's sport (Bairner, 2001). National cultures are formed and transformed in relation to specific social relations and may at times be 'imagined' or reinvented, these processes mean that national identity is not fixed but fluid (Maguire, 1993). In particular, dominant groups construct identities about the nation through stories, often invented, which reflect or reinforce their ideas about the nation. This was the case in the transformation of cricket from a violent sport to a sport which was considered to embody qualities of fair play, valour and gentlemanly conduct. This was a habitus particularly associated with upper-class gentlemanliness, through reimagining the game, cricket came to embody or represent what it meant to be English at a specific time (Maguire, 1993). In addition cricket often reflects a tendency to romanticise the past and the dominance of England in the Empire. Yet for those who were colonised, and in countries where cricket became a dominant sport, cricket came to reflect struggles between England and those countries that had been under British rule. In particular, beating the mother country came to symbolise struggle and the development of national identities and character in specific countries. For example, in Australia cricket became a vehicle for the forging of a national identity that sought to oppose the mother country (Maguire, 1993). Yet parts of these national identities are invented traditions and stories which serve to reinforce types of national identities that become dominant (and are largely based on masculinity and masculine national identities). However, in all instances, cricket was reinvented to capture a sense of national identity and masculinity. As part of this war-like imagery is used when describing matches such as The Ashes and the desire to 'beat' the mother country at its own game. This draws on masculinity and notions of colonialism and brutality associated with war and masculinity to describe a sporting event. As sports have become increasingly globalised, the balance between local, global and national identities is simultaneously weakened and strengthened and through such processes. Maguire (2011) suggests that the relationship between sport, identity policies and 'wilful nostalgia' should be considered.

Modern sport as identified in many texts was created for men, and through the development of sport and the nation the legacies of masculinity and sport are well established. In particular, global flows and labour migration are highly gendered despite there being little research in this area. In Chapter 3, I noted how women have always supported cricket and women are part of the 'nation' which celebrates male cricketing success as it is male cricketers who embody this sense of nationalism and it is their success that nations celebrate. Women, both presently and historically, have supported male national cricket teams and largely accept this form of national identity, although little is known about female sport fandom and how females identify with the nation through supporting male sports teams. When female fans are considered, they are often viewed as new consumers of sport and a new commercial market to sell sports materials, whereas women have a long tradition of fandom and identification with the nation through sport (Pope, 2011). As Maguire (2012: 156) clearly identified, 'Male sport appears to play a crucial role in the construction and representation of English national identity.' I would argue that a similar sentiment can be found in the construction of national identity more broadly. It is predominantly male sport that reflects the nation and the role of the sport–media nexus has reinforced these elements of sport, national identity and cricket. The relationship between cricket, the nation and masculine national identities is critical in reinforcing ideas about women as the outsider group within the cricket figuration.

Other research in this area is slight, one of the few, Stevenson (2002), illustrates that most of the nation's sporting heroes are men and it is largely men who represent the nation in certain sports. There are some differences, for example, in tennis and athletics, in which gender and nation are more closely identified with. However, largely in team sports and specifically in sports like cricket, football and rugby, the relationship between the nation and masculinity is particularly strong and this arguably influences the social habitus of those females who play for the nation and the value of their involvement is arguably less than it is for male cricketers. The purpose of this chapter is to explore the experiences of women who play cricket at elite levels of the game (all were currently playing for their national team) from across the globe, drawing on interview data from current elite national players. This first section considers how the social identities of those who play the game are influenced by wider established and outsider relations. Secondly, the chapter draws on data from members of the England Women's Cricket Association (EWCA) at the time of the merger with the England and Wales Cricket Board (ECB) and ten years on to explore the role of mergers in the shifting social identities of female cricketers, considering the changing dynamics and the social habitus of the established and outsider groups in such figurations. In the following section I draw on interviews with current players who play for their nation drawing on key themes that are part of these global experiences.

Women's global experiences of cricket

Playing with the boys

Nearly all the women involved in the interviews had played during their careers cricket either formally or informally with boys. This is largely because for many girls, cricket structures do not exist for girls to play the game, and so many play on boys' teams or with male relatives as the only introduction to playing cricket. For example, Player 1 from South Africa suggests, 'Trying to find a girls' team to play in was next to impossible . . . I just played with the boys.' Player 3 (England) recalls, 'I started playing for a boys' team with my older brother, where my mum and dad were involved with the club', and Player 1 (Australia) noted that she 'started playing at eight years in the local boys' team with my brother'. Interestingly the role of playing with boys was quite common, and even Player 2 from India recalls that she trained with her elder brother in the nets. For many girls and women, men are the gatekeepers to their involvement in the game. The lack of formal structures for girls to be involved in the game means that girls and women often rely on support from male relatives or through being allowed to play on boys' or male teams to have their first experience of playing cricket. The lack of formal structures for girls to play the game is the first indication for females that cricket is more closely associated with a male habitus than a female one.

The experience of those girls and women who play on boys' cricket teams is varied. For some it can put them off the game as they feel excluded, whilst for others it can be a form of support: 'It's fine they respect me' (Player 1, England); 'Once they see a girl can play to a serious standard they are quite welcoming' (Player 2, England). Playing with boys does however raise some issues for some girls as deep-seated ideological beliefs about the capabilities of males and females in the game exist. In all cases because men and boys are the established group in numerical dominance, longevity of association and a more closely bonded character, male cricketers can continue to dominate or control women's and girls' access to the sport as well. Through such close interdependencies, the established group is able to infer through forms of gossip the girls' outsider status, and for many girls and women, playing cricket is not a right or not a normal part of school structures of childhood experiences; so from an early age, their identity as a female cricketer perceived by others as unusual.

The identity of a female cricketer as a cricketer is an unusual habitus and the lack of formal cricketing structures, lack of female teams and general lack of media coverage mean that from an early age females internalise the belief that cricket is a male sport. This is largely the case in all the countries in which women played elite cricket.

Financial support and monopolisation of key resources

One of the continuing issues for elite female cricketers who represent their country is financial support. The teams have varying levels of support for female cricket and there is a lot of disparity between male and female cricketers' pay. Historically, as seen throughout this book, women who play cricket and represent the nation have done so voluntarily and often had to pay to travel and play the game. With the shift in governance from the International Women's Cricket Council (IWCC) to the International Cricket Council (ICC) and the merging of national organisations, there is more money in the women's game. There remains varying financial support for female cricketers. One recent example of this discussed in media reports is at the recent ICC World Cup, where it was revealed that English female players had a daily allowance of £37 whereas male cricketers had an allowance of £62 (Williamson, 2012). The allowance paid by the ECB sends a clear message that women are valued less for doing the same job. (This was not about prize money or pay, but expenses, which are the same for each player regardless of gender and such disparity in pay is not clear.) Interestingly the English women were more successful than the men in this tournament, so even when more successful, women are granted lower living costs for playing cricket. Such media reports are often responded to with the argument that women receive less sponsorship, gate money and commercial rights (i.e. television coverage), yet these arguments fail to recognise that women are also representing their nation and these expenses are related to daily costs so the reasoning behind different amounts is not entirely clear. In nearly all of the ICC full membership countries, men are paid to play cricket and can earn a living from playing cricket. In many cases, this is possible even if they do not represent the national side. Additional financial support can come from leagues such as the Indian Premier League that have become lucrative for male cricketers. Financial support for female cricketers is not a given. In the West Indies some women are now on central contracts, which means that this can support players; in England central contracts do exist for some players; and in Australia as well, some players have central contracts. The nature of these vary; in some cases women are expected to work in coaching to maintain these contracts and some contracts are not enough for players to live off.

In New Zealand the players' interviews identified that levels of financial reward are not enough to sustain players and that most players work as well as play cricket for their country. Player 3 notes, 'I have a job, its full time. . . . Getting time off work financially, I don't recoup what I lose by taking unpaid leave.' Player 2 also explains, 'I have a full time job . . . the challenges are getting time off to attend training camps.' Different national governing bodies have adopted different strategies for trying to increase financial support through a variety of means. In India women cricketers are generally employed to work for national companies such as Indian Railways or Air India. This is a historic trend which has continued to support players, but such contracts of work are real, as Player 2 from India explains: 'We play for the company and the country.' Women working for the companies are still expected to fulfil their work duties, as she later explains: 'There are deadlines you need to meet and it is important to give 100% to your job that is your bread earner.' Thus having to commit to the company and playing for India both require 100% commitment.

In England, women who play for the national side are paid for tours and match fees and 50% of players also have a contract with Chance to Shine (a cricket charity). The Chance to Shine contracts are a way for women to commit to playing the game, but as part of the contract, players have to do a number of hours of community coaching or school coaching, as Player 2 from England explains:

> It was a great opportunity as it was hard to find suitable employment which allowed the flexibility to play. Challenges were often felt tired, as you do a whole day of work and still have to then do a full training session.

The structure differs in Australia with central contracts. In Australia there are different tiers in relation to how much players are paid (which seems to differ per player). Player 1 suggests the amount offered in contracts is 'not enough to live off'; these tiers and contracts are in addition to tour allowances, but despite this, most players continue to work elsewhere to support their involvement in cricket. As a member of a team representing the 'nation', this can pose difficulties, as Player 5 from Australia notes: 'I have to take leave without pay . . . I know women who have lost their job because of the demands of cricket.' Playing for the nation can be costly. Cricketers in South Africa appear the least well supported, and at present, as Player 1 from South Africa makes it clear, 'there is no means of making a living from cricket in South Africa'.

Despite the lack of pay, the women's game is professional in all other regards. This poses questions around what constitutes a professional sport and how professional sport is defined as definitions of professional sport tend to focus on being 'paid'. However, as Dunning (1999) highlights, different forms of sport professionalism exist but legitimate forms of sports professionalism include financial support through sponsorship or ticket money and financial support given by media for broadcasting matches. In this regard women's cricket could be classified as legitimately professional in that the women's game does sell tickets and does receive sponsorship and broadcasting (through the ICC and other organisations) and there is prize money for the winners of ICC international tournaments. Yet the prize money for tournaments remains far more for men than for women, as Table 5.1 shows.

The ICC has been criticised by some for this disparity in prize money, which continues to reinforce the view that the male game

Table 5.1   ICC World T20 prize money

Men's prize money	
Winner	$1,100,000
Runner-up	$550,000
Semifinalists	$275,000 (×2)
Group (R2) match win	$40,000 (×20 matches)
Women's prize money	
Winner	$70,000
Runner-up	$30,000
Semifinalist	$15,000 (×2)
Group match win	$2,500 (×20 matches = $50,000)

Source: ICC, 2014.

is the established form of the game and is the game that brings in commercial and sponsorship opportunities. Some male teams receive more media coverage and larger audiences but they are not paid differently. The ICC decides how much cricketers receive from prize money; this perhaps illustrates some of the continuing inequalities that female cricketers face in the modern game. Women do not tend to openly ask for better financial rewards from an established group. It is the established group that continues to judge the value of the women's game and whether it can compare to the men's game. Whereas in reality the women's game is starting from a different position, historically underfunded, with teams that are semiprofessional or amateur and with little media coverage, which impacts on whether people are even aware of the women's game. In this respect power relations continue to be related to the monopolisation of resources and the inequality of pay can be justified by the established group who judge the outsiders as less worthy of equity in relation to pay. Here the arguments about whether it is moral to continue to pay women less may become more apparent, as media or others lobby for better pay for female cricketers (similar to tennis), through greater interdependency with the established group. Increased mutual identification may enable women to challenge the continuing discrepancy in pay and support, the moral indignation brought on those organisations that continue to deny support to women may arouse embarrassment and claims of uncivilised behaviour in not supporting women's cricket may enable women opportunities to gain (albeit slowly) better access to financial resources.

Most elite female cricketers who play for their country cannot make a living from playing cricket and the pay for winning tournaments remains minimal. In this respect, women are professionals in terms of the amount of tours they compete in and training they complete but in terms of being paid this continues to be varied. They play international competitions, but definitions of global, professional and national sports seem to be highly gendered and as Player 3 from New Zealand illustrates:

> There is a greater requirement for players time and commitment but players don't get paid to train and play and have a career. A lot of players' careers have been limited.

Thus for female cricketers, the opportunities to make money from playing cricket are limited. This is a double-edged sword as often their careers are affected by their playing cricket, so in both cases they are compromised.

Women, cricket and sport migration

Female cricketers have travelled overseas to play cricket since the first tour in 1934, and women have played cricket in different countries and played seasons for different counties in the UK and in the Cricket Week; for example, in women's cricket magazines, there are numerous examples of migration. When Australia toured England in 1963, many players stayed to play in the infamous Cricket Week and were involved in playing in teams. Sport migration for women remains an underresearched area (Botelho and Agergaard, 2011). One of the reasons for this is that sport labour migration has often been considered as being part of global and economic forces and these are not always appropriate for considering labour sport migration in women's sport. Maguire suggests a typology for sport migrants with the following categories: pioneers, settlers, mercenaries, nomadic cosmopolitans and returnees (in Botelho and Agergaard, 2011). As Botelho and Agergaard (2011) identify, such typologies are derived largely from research on male sports, and the authors suggest an approach which considers less rational motives for migration as female sport migration is not driven by the same forces as men's sport labour migration. The authors suggest drawing on the work of Freidson on *'Labour of Love'* as a more useful framework of analysis as many female migrants are not motivated by monetary gain. In this study, for the women interviewed there was evidence of migration, but not for money; in fact for some women migration was costly. Player 1 from Australia had played in England for Staffordshire County: 'I loved it, it helped me rediscover my love for the game.' Player 5 from Australia had played in New Zealand in its national competition and played for Otago whilst coming back from injury. This player had also played for Berkshire in England for a summer. West Indies Player 1 played in Australia for three months for a club, and this was funded by the Jamaica Cricket Association, illustrating that the organisation must have valued the opportunity of having players in other countries, maybe for playing experience or coaching. Player 3 from New Zealand had had an opportunity to play in Australia for Brisbane and she paid for this opportunity herself and her motivation for paying for this opportunity was because she benefitted from 'understanding the different training other countries do that helped me with my game'; 'I had the opportunity to play for Tasmania, but due to work commitments this didn't happen.' Player 1 from England had played cricket for Port Adelaide in Australia and she noted that it was a great opportunity to 'develop my game independently'; she partly funded this herself with some monetary support for flights from the Surrey Men's Academy. Sport 'labour' migration in the women's game was limited mainly by a lack of financial support to be able to play. Women who did play in other countries did for the desire to experience playing cricket in another country; this is largely symptomatic of the women's game in which there is no benefit to 'migrating' for financial purposes. The players from India and Pakistan who were interviewed from this study had not experienced migration to play cricket, which may signal some continuing inequalities in terms of freedom of movement (i.e. visas and financial issues). Unlike Botelho and Agergaard (2011), whose research explored female professional footballers' experiences where there was some financial gain available, in women's cricket there is no money associated with cricket migration. Thus similar to Botelho and Agergaard (2011), there is a need to understand a global exchange even when money and media attention are low and this suggests a broader understanding of sports migration might be needed to capture the experience of female sport migrants who move or travel to experience their sport without any financial gain.

Functional democratisation and social habitus of individuals

Opportunities for female cricketers to play the sport have undoubtedly increased. The major global tournaments such as the ICC World Cup and ICC T20 have increased the visibility of women's cricket. The development of cricket for women in the national governing bodies highlights a varying picture in relation to women's opportunities to play the game. In this section, I consider how the mergers at the organisational level impact on the habitus and identities of the outsider groups, in other words, when the established and outsider groups are more interdependent, how the identity of the outsider group is affected by these complex figurations.

Functional democratisation and the impact of mergers on the outsider group

All the women interviewed noted a difference in the level of the women's game since the mergers with relevant male cricketing authorities. This suggests that the level of competition had increased; for example, Player 2 from India stresses that 'the media has started following the women's game as well and they keep a tab on the proceedings – domestic and international'. Player 1 from Australia suggests that 'more international games [are] being played across the world which helps improve the standard of the game'. The higher standard of the games was mentioned by Player 2 from Australia: 'Batting over time has improved – girls [are] stronger and hit bigger.' The structure of cricket at national levels had also enabled competitive matches to be played more frequently, thus increasing the level of play. Player 4 from Australia suggests that the professionalisation of the sport has enabled 'better access to facilities, coaches and grounds', but this did differ in different national structures; Player 1 from South Africa notes that there needs to be more 'structures in place for a girl to join a team', as the structures can prevent progression. Player 1 from Pakistan notes that 'there is not a very strong financial structure of women's cricket in Pakistan and we don't play international matches more often'. She later goes on to explain that a lack of domestic cricket tournaments can impact on the game and the development of competitive cricket. Those countries that had had an established cricketing structure prior to the merger with their male cricketing body appear to have had more stability and increased growth than those with newer governing bodies like Pakistan. The differing levels of support can impact on the global game as Player 2 from New Zealand suggests: 'Countries not investing money in the same way are falling behind and highlighting a gap between semi-professional and amateur nations.' Whilst the ICC as the global governing body can encourage the development of the global game, the development of national sides is more impacted by the national governing bodies, and apart from the ICC policy that insisted on gender mainstreaming of national governing bodies, a systematic approach to ensuring gender equity in these organisations is not addressed, nor do there appear to be any sanctions for those who do not demonstrate gender equity.

Given the changes to the structure of women's cricket and the merging of the IWCC and ICC alongside the merging of national organisations, it suggests that in the established and outsider figuration of women's cricket, the established and outsider groups have become more interdependent, and women's cricketers are now an integral part of the global game (although there continue to be some discrepancies in this regard). The changing position of women's cricket was discussed by those involved in the game. Some women challenged the position of women's cricket, suggesting that more needed to be done to promote the game, especially around financial rewards in the game; some identified the role of the media in promoting the women's game: 'more games on TV which will help with the increase of media all round and increased financial support (Player 1, Australia), 'increased financial reward for playing was essential for the development of the game', 'women having more contracts' (Player 1, Australia), and 'female cricketers to have more financial support to eventually one day be full time athletes' (Player 1, Australia). On the other hand, some women players were more careful about considering their position in the cricket figuration, poised between resistance and resignation, and were therefore careful to be perceived as being grateful for current improvements in the game and were careful not to appear too demanding of new structures: 'I am extremely grateful for the support that my work provides me with' (Player 3, Australia).

Issues such as women and families and careers were also brought up by the women who suggested that this may impact on women's opportunities: 'Women have to think about a career or starting a family. You can't do both playing and competing and working at the highest level' (Player 4, Australia). Such comments draw on established notions of how women combine families, work and playing for the nation, which creates challenges for the outsider group. For some females, the support given is not something to be expected when playing for your nation, but something that should be considered lucky to have: 'We are lucky there is a lot of support from the media' (Player 2, England). Likewise Player 1 from West Indies notes, 'We get a fair amount of support from the local media which is lovely.' In these comments are still ideas that suggest an outsider group charisma, one that is largely accepting of the current position, seeing it as an inevitable and a part of being involved in a sport that is largely dominated by men. For Player 1 from New Zealand, 'at the end of the day it is a privilege to represent your country'. It is highly unlikely that male players would say the same about playing for their country if they were not' paid, juggling working life, training and struggling; the outsiders continue to be wary about criticising the male established group, largely accepting their group disgrace as a type of harmonious inequality. The self-image of females does not appear to challenge the dominance of the established group and the women are 'poised between resignation and resistance' (Van Stolk and Wouters, 1987: 479). As Player 1 from New Zealand says, the men's and women's games are different and the women's game will not receive the same levels of support as the men's game:

> We need to treat it differently to the men's game. It will never reach the same success financially as the guys and if we always have a focus we will always come up short.

Player 4 also critiques the current structures, in which women play at international matches as warm-ups for the men's game; she suggests, 'I would like to see the women's game continue to develop in a way that we don't need to play in men's competition to be noticed.' The path for the development of the women's game is contentious and the focus on not being warm-up matches for the men's game is not one universally popular and may encourage the comparison of men's and women's cricket in a way that is not favourable for the women's game.

One of the continuing issues in the women's cricket is something that has not received much academic attention in general and is about the continuing relationship between cricket and nationalism, national identity and gender. In all the cases discussed, cricket continues to reinforce national identity and masculinity, and there is little evidence at present to consider whether women's cricket can reflect the national identity of those involved in the nation; that is, can the success of the women's game result in pride and loss result in shame and humiliation of the nation? At present academically, the nation and the link between the nation and national identity in cricket literature is presented as male. As Marjoribanks and Farquharson (2012: 79) identify when discussing Australian cricket, while both men's and women's national teams are very successful, it is the men's team that gains the overwhelming majority of attention and praise in the context of nation-building.

This is inextricably linked to the sport–media nexus in which media representations of sport and the nation are still closely associated with male sport, especially in the context of cricket and the nations discussed in this text, and there is little evidence that women's sport, is 'a site for the symbolic binding of the people of the country through culture'; this seems especially the case in women's sport and women team sports. There is some difference in media and national identity in mega events such as the Olympics, where men and women compete in the same competition, but these events are historically for men and women competitors and there are differences in media representations between men and women athletes in these sports (Mansfield and Curtis, 2009). In team sports, especially those with close links to the nation and masculinity like cricket, the relationship between sport and national identity is not fully understood. Another underresearched area is the role of women as sports fans more broadly. Women attend and support male teams; for example, the Barmy Army, an organised group of English cricket fans (with over 5,000 members), who support the male cricket team, have a section on 'Barmy Girls' which must indicate that a number of the Barmy Army who support the male team are female. Although the organisation is predominantly male, the social identity of these fans and gender relations are unclear. Women are part of the nation and they play sports while representing the nation but their victories (or defeats) do not reinforce the 'sense of nation'. Thus research in this area has largely ignored the relationship between gender relations, sport, nation states and nation building.

Mergers, social identities and the role of women in interdependent relations

In this section I explore research conducted on female cricketers and the impact of the merger on cricket in England. This research draws on the views of key women involved in the EWCA at the time of the merger with the ECB and their views on the merger ten years after the event. I draw on data obtained by conversations with 10 women who had been involved in the EWCA organisation/structure to explore the perceptions of women involved not only in the playing but crucially in the development and structure/organisation of the game. This is presented as a case study for understanding power relations and social habituses of individuals during phases emancipation. As discussed in Chapter 4, certain preconditions and wider changes in power relations enabled the mergers to take place at the time in which they did.

In discussing the aims of merger, the women noted that there were several reasons for deciding to merge with the ECB. These were predominantly financial, for example, and for the existing structures that the ECB had:

> The world was changing too quickly. Professionalisation, money, and the whole Sport England that was driving 4 year plans. (EWCA Member 1)

> It was really financial, . . . we never had that before it was money, monetary support and equal opportunity. (EWCA Member 6)

There was some expectation that the merger would bring with it increased opportunities for the development of the women's game, as one key member of the EWCA said:

> It just being where cricket was and becoming part of cricket per se, without having to be called men's cricket or women's cricket. It's just cricket and I feel that is where it should be. (EWCA Member 3)

As the EWCA had depended on volunteers for so long, the organisation had struggled to develop a sustainable structure that was fragile as the lack of paid positions meant there were difficulties in establishing a structure:

> It became evident there were very few people involved in the running of it . . . what seemed apparent to me was that people played the sport and got involved for a period of time, but then they might have gone away to have kids or do other things and suddenly that would be lost, there wasn't a formal structure there. The structure was based on the good old volunteer. (EWCA Member 8)

The EWCA was in a position in which finically and structurally the organisation was struggling to develop, and it had become stagnant;

however members also point to the pressure to merge and also the relationship between men's cricket and access to funding, which could be gained through a merger:

> To get lottery funding for one of their stands, admitting women was part of the deal . . . they wanted the grant but they were a rich enough club and they could have done it without the grant so they weren't railroaded . . . I think it was more political to acknowledge equal opportunities law. (EWCA Member 3)

The access to funding was seen as a potential power resource to the women, as it gave them a reason for why the ECB would want to merge. This alongside pressure for equal opportunities and new policies enabled women to signal that the merger was needed, and there was a mixed view of the merger amongst men and women cricketers.

> The view they only want is there because they might get some funding and they are just paying lip service to us . . . it became apparent quickly that there was going to be greater opposition from the women than there was from the men. (EWCA Member 4)

The opposition to the merger amongst the outsider group demonstrates that whilst some wanted greater interdependency with the established group, others did not want this and wanted to continue to be separate – the reason being fear of a loss of identity and loss of control over the game. In these accounts, the objection to the merger seems to be related to the fact that control over the game was seen to be given to the established group, and given the lack of support given to the game, this was a concern as the women were worried the established group did not understand the women's game, the structures, the international game and the current structures that enabled a governing body to develop the game since 1926. In essence the motivations of the established group were also of concern to the outsider group; although they knew that the women's game was struggling, they considered that control over the game was a critical part of the game. For others there was a view that the increased visibility of just being there would aid the women's game:

> They would see us every day so they can't actually forget us, that it becomes part of everybody's role within the organisation to

consider and take on women and girls cricket and to promote it and support it. (EWCA Member 4)

This view of integration and visibility seems to draw on the notion of increased interdependency, the idea that just being visible is important for the consideration of women's cricket; that is, it could no longer just be ignored because it would be part of a wider organisation and integrated as part of that organisation. However, whether visibility is enough to secure the outcomes that the women want for the game in a new structure is not entirely clear.

One of the things that did change significantly after the merger between the EWCA and the ECB was the role of women within an organisation, particularly women's role within positions of power and authority in the game. One of these roles is coaching. In the EWCA, the coaching was done predominantly by women, as were the committee roles and other roles such as umpiring. These roles were performed by women; women completed advanced coaching courses and held awards such as the MCC Advanced Coaching certificate, and were therefore considered qualified coaches and therefore women were instrumental in coaching the game. However this changed when the merger happened, as:

In the early stuff it was all women coaches, more latterly men became involved. I think that might reflect that coaching was starting to become a career opportunity and it was men who were taking those opportunities. (EWCA Member 2)

Opportunities to be involved in paid coaching becomes more associated with men; perhaps an unintended consequence of the process of increased interdependence between the established and the outsider is that more paid opportunities arise, yet these opportunities tend to be monopolised by the established group. For some the involvement of male coaches was seen by some as unnecessary, as for example EWCA Member 3 notes:

We won the World Cup in 73 with the WCA and we won it again in 93 (with female coaches and manager).

Thus the employment of the established group in positions of power in the women's game can be viewed by the outsider group as the established group capitalising on opportunities that had previously been for women. It is men who have largely benefitted from the increasing number of opportunities to work within cricket, and this can cause issues with the outsider group, as EWCA Member 9 states:

> They are being coached by coaches who haven't had anything to do with women's cricket largely, many of them haven't probably seen a game of women's cricket.

Thus rather than opportunities rising for women coaches to increase their involvement in cricket overall, women involved in key positions consider that their involvement in the women's game has decreased and no further opportunities have arisen for women to be involved either through coaching or organisationally in the men's game. 'It was run by women. We did all the training' (EWCA Member 1). This is summed up by EWCA Member 6 when she notes:

> This is one of the things we lost out on. Women have lost out in coaching jobs and umpiring.

This sense of loss is not uncommon when male and female sporting organisations merge (Hoeber, 2007). This feeling of loss was echoed in the organisation of the game more broadly, as EWCA Member 2 notes: 'It did change things, the EWCA was like a family.' The sense of a loss of identity was felt more when those involved reflected on the merger ten years on:

> Losing control on how things were organised and not necessarily being able to resist change . . . and yeah I suppose losing their own identity and control. (EWCA Member 10)

This may reflect a feeling of wilful nostalgia, but during this time the pace of change was not always what was expected by the outsider group. Those changes in the game were not always viewed positively, as mentioned in the introductory chapter; the role of the Ashes was discussed as an ongoing issue:

> We would have never agreed to water it down to one match, it is a three-match series it's the Ashes for God's sake. (EWCA Member 6)

The view that the Ashes are meaningful is critical here, as the view is that the Ashes should be taken seriously as an event that captures tradition. Test match cricket more broadly was viewed as problematic and something that was considered to have declined since the merger:

> It undermines the women's game, it is meaningless, it is the only test match women play. (EWCA Member 6)

Thus greater interdependence organisationally was not always considered a positive move for the women's game and is summed up by EWCA Member 9 who notes: 'I term it invisible integration, so integrated you can't actually see it. They talk the talk so it looks like it is happening.'

Outsider groups and group fragmentation

One of the criticisms of the theory of established and outsider relations (Bloyce and Murphy, 2007) is the seemingly stagnant and fixed nature of the terms 'established' and 'outsider', which are seemingly static and against Eliasian concepts of process. Whilst the terms are linguistically static they capture or refer to processes. For example, the outsider group is fragmented and the relations between the established and outsider group are based on a number of processes(Dunning, 1999; Mennell, 1992). In their seminal paper on the use of the theory as a concept to explore power relations between the sexes, Van Stolk and Wouters (1987) illustrate the social conditions of being an outsider group in a figuration, undergoing significant changes in power relations towards equalisation. These tend to result in different social attitudes towards equalisation of relations and they describe outsider groups as falling into several categorises in this regard: the radicals, the moderates and the stragglers. Firstly, the radicals are able to develop their own 'we' identity and are proud of it. Secondly, the moderates tend to want the old stigmas removed. Finally, the stragglers prefer old behavioural patterns, yet they may feel pressured by the ideas of the liberation movement (Van Stolk and Wouters, 1987). This illuminates that outsider groups are fragmented, with differing perceptions of the move towards equalisation. In relation to the EWCA, there was some difference in relation to the 'perception' and 'image' of women's cricket that highlights some of the tensions between female cricketers and the need to present an image that the established group would support:

> You are presenting an image, that the whole world is looking at . . . you know relationships . . . one thing that we were very clear about is that we didn't want it. (EWCA Member 5)

The discussion about sexuality and media image is not uncommon in female sport, as one member discusses a comment she heard at the ECB about the merger:

> You'll have to get the dykes on board, and I think that is how they saw it, that sporting women were probably lesbian. (EWCA Member 3)

Such comments serve to demonstrate the power of stigmatisation of outsider groups and how stigma is socially created in established and outsider groups as well as in considering how established and out-sider groups can use stigma as a way of creating group disgrace/group charisma. The perception of female sports women as 'gay' is some-thing that both the EWCA and, through the merger, the ECB have tried to counter; for example, as EWCA Member 8 notes:

> People might think the same thing about women who play sports – that they are all gay . . . I don't know if that has changed since the merger or anything like that, but if you look, there is a lot more lip gloss than there used to be . . . they present the glamorous side and it's pretty wholesome.

The view is that sexuality is something that can be identified through appearance; that is, it is the way a woman looks (heterosexual and attractive to men) that enables the diffusion of the image of women who play masculine sport as homosexual, but the fact that the per-ception or the attitude to homosexual women in the sport is consid-ered something that the sport needs to manage is both problematic and something that is continually policed in women's sport, as het-eronormativity is in part linked to male dominance more broadly (Marjoribanks and Farquharson, 2012).

Through reflecting on the merger, there was also a sense that certain women at certain levels, particularly at elite levels, of the game had benefitted from 'sponsorship and grants' (EWCA Member 1). But one of the issues is related to the real information about the numbers of women playing against the numbers actually playing; for example, EWCA Member 1 notes:

> All the counties have development officers, whose job is to teach cricket to young people, so they have to teach girls as well as boys. So theoretically there should be whole new markets of players and if you read the stats there are . . . but I don't believe a word of it, they count a kid in primary school who has a kwik cricketer experience.

The appointment of Taunton as the home of women's cricket in England was also considered problematic, not only because it is a minority ground, but also because of its location in the country which makes it difficult for all to access. These issues illustrated the extent to which women had gone into the merger as the weaker partners and their ability to challenge this was difficult:

> I have a feeling they were the only county who volunteered . . . it is a bit out of a limb, but beggars can't be choosers can they? (EWCA Member 7)

The mergers therefore represent a form of functional democratisation in that they demonstrate a reduction in power imbalances and greater interdependence between the established and the outsider group. But in joining an organisation with substantially more 'players' and joining as a much weaker entity, the women felt they could no longer control the development of women's cricket. Increased funding and focusing on elite levels has unintended consequences for the women's game, in which there is a feeling that the grass roots of the game is not developing as it should. The second issue is the increasing role of the established group in controlling or developing the women's game in ways that benefit the established group, that is, creating coaching jobs. Thus women's roles in the organisation and structure of the game has significantly changed since the mergers of the EWCA and ECB – and ultimately the IWCC and ICC – and the role of women in global organisations in management positions continues to be limited.

Recently, 16 years after the merger with the ECB, England women cricketers have now been funded through central contracts with the ECB. The first 18 women cricketers to be awarded central England contracts have been named by the ECB. This is part of a wider promise by the ECB to significantly reinvest in the women's game. In discussing the reasoning behind why this decision had been made, the ECB noted the success of the team. Interestingly this still identifies a difference between men's and women's cricket, with men being funded regardless of their success or defeat. Thus whilst women have to justify their payments as mentioned in a recent *BBC* article, the women are receiving the funding because they 'unequivocally justify the financial reward which comes with the new England women's contracts' (*BBC Sport*, 2014). Yet for male cricketers who play at such levels, such justification is rarely expected.

This shift to central funding does identify that changes at organisational levels do not ensure equity; social processes involved in changing social habituses are important to consider in these changes. It is only through being part of the organisational networks over a period of time that female cricketers in England are increasingly able to gain access to resources that enable them to develop the game and, moreover, attitudes are much slower to change in this regard. In the seminal paper by Van Stolk and Wouters (1987), in which they mention different groups of outsiders during emancipation phases, they mention the difference between radicals, moderates and stragglers. Something similar may be evident in the established group, with some of the established group, through their increasing interdependency and mutual identification with the outsider group, being more radical in supporting the outsiders than others who continue to consider the women as outsiders who should 'justify their position' within the figuration; of course such justification only serves to emphasise women's outsider status by highlighting their difference, and inferiority, by directly comparing the women's game to the men's game, when such comparisons inevitably disadvantage the women's game.

Concluding thoughts

In exploring the development of the international governance of women's cricket, it is possible to also consider the more micro aspects of the game in relation to the experiences of women who play the global game. Thus considering how structures and social processes influence social habituses of those playing cricket, drawing on the experiences of current players of the game in a variety of national contexts, further supports the notion of a civilising direction in the women's game. This is evidenced by more opportunities to play the global game; alongside this is better, albeit not equal, pay. More women are financially supported to play. For example, some players have central contracts offered to allow them to play full time. However, in some cases this does not come with payment which would enable women cricketers to support themselves whilst playing for the 'nation'. There continue to be extensive differences in different nations as to the level of support given to women who represent their nation. Women's cricket is increasingly professionalised in its approach but this raises significant questions about what constitutes professionalism, as many cricketers also have a career that supports them as they play the game; thus they struggle to commit fully to either cricket or their career and both are jeopardised. The announcement by the ECB to have the first fully professional cricket team will bring with it other responsibilities that women cricketers may not have faced before, with increased media scrutiny that may heighten group disgrace.

In considering the merger of male and female organisations, here it becomes apparent how changes at organisational levels influence the social habitus of the members of the outsider group. The mergers represent an interesting shift in power balances in which women's cricket is recognised by the established group. These organisational changes are not always supported by a fragmented outsider group, who are wary of the motivations of the established group and their intentions once the organisations have merged. Furthermore, in the merger there are changes in relation to the roles that women have within the organisational networks of the game as women have less of a role in these organisations than they previously did and such mergers have enabled men to be more involved in the provision and ultimately have more control over the development of women's cricket. For instance, strategically women's cricket is planned through central organisations that may have little previous knowledge or understanding of the game, women lose their autonomy and for some outsider groups this loss of autonomy over the organisation is seen as a loss of female identity in shaping the women's game. In this chapter, I have drawn specifically on England as a case study, but other studies such as that by Stronach and Adair (2009) have researched the merger in Australia and found similar issues. In Australia, the merger happened in 2003, with similar issues being identified as a reason for the merger, namely lack of finances and development. The Australian Women's Cricket Council (AWCC) was having significant issues with sponsorship and merger in 2003 and the women's game was embraced in strategic plans, including the overall mission to ensure that cricket becomes Australia's national sport (Stronach and Adair, 2009). From their research, Stronach and Adair (2009) identify that women within the AWCC were concerned privately about the merger, expressing similar concerns to the EWCA about loss of identity and history. In both contexts, it is clear that one of the ongoing inequities between men and women in organisational structures is with women sitting on the boards of both the ECB and Cricket Australia where women do not often sit on these influential decision-making boards. In the Australian context, this lack of female representation seems to be at odds with the current position in government, suggesting an issue with sporting boards. As Stronach and Adair (2009) identify in particular in sporting governing bodies, this seems to an ongoing issue and is reported elsewhere in the literature on gender and governing bodies (Hoeber, 2007; Thompson, 1990). In Australia, there is an attempt to address this through policy and legalisation as otherwise such change may not occur. Women's continuing lack of influence or position in managerial roles is clearly an example of continuing power imbalances between men's and women's cricket, and sport more broadly.

Through the merging of organisations, men have had more involvement in the game, and instead of a partnership emerging, in both cases the women's cricket had to fit in with the men's game. One further unintended consequence of these mergers is clearly highlighted in the case study of the merger between the EWCA and ECB, which is that men have had increasing opportunity to coach, manage and umpire within the women's game. These coaching and managerial positions have often created increasing opportunities for men to be employed in cricket, whilst decreasing the opportunities for women who used to coach, manage and umpire the game. In being in the governing body of the women's game, men have had the opportunity to develop the game in line with the established group (whether this is intentional or not); women's strategic development of the game is decided by the established group and this may be at odds with the needs and desires of a fragmented outsider group that wants to see the women's game develop differently than it has and for some women, this alienates them from the game.

In the concluding chapter, I reflect further on a figurational analysis of the issues discussed in the book and consider the adoption of a figurational framework for the analysis of gender relations and long-term social processes, as well as concluding by identifying current issues in the global women's game by identifying the changing elements of international women's cricket that both enable and constrain its continual development.

6
Conclusion

The aim of *Women's Cricket and Global Processes: The Emergence and Development of Women's Cricket as a Global Game* 'has been to develop a sociological analysis of the emergence and development of women's cricket as a global game, and in particular, to offer a sociological analysis of the social processes that influenced the emergence and development of women's cricket. In doing so, the book has sought to make visible women cricketers in academic and establishment accounts of cricket research and to demonstrate that women's cricket is and has been for some time an international and global game. Women have been involved not only in playing cricket but also as spectators and supporters of men's cricket, women have always supported cricket, 'watching since the dawn of cricket, in dreadful proximity to the bat' (Joy 1950: 13). Gender relations in cricket have not been extensively discussed in historical and academic accounts of the game and gender relations are often not considered a feature of the modern game, yet this book clearly outlines how the relationship between cricket, masculinity and the nation is a defining feature of the global modern game.

Theoretical considerations

As mentioned in the introduction to this book', a figurational approach to this topic may be unusual given the criticism levelled at figurational sociology and its perceived focus on male sport (Hargreaves, 1992, 1994). It is not my intention to suggest that figurational sociology is the only way to study gender relations in cricket but rather to present a figurational approach to such an analysis, which seeks to explain the emergence and development of women's cricket through considering a relational approach (i.e. how did women's cricket emerge and develop in relation to men's cricket?) and through considering diffusion processes more broadly, as well as through critically considering the relationship between cricket, the nation and masculinity which has both enabled and constrained the development of women's cricket. Fundamentally, at the heart of this analysis is the figurational approach: 'Only by examining how things have come to be that we can adequately understand their contemporary form' (Malcolm, 2013: 14). It is clear that through considering men's cricket, cricket was associated with masculinity, and in particular it is a sport that comes to reflect and reinforce a type of masculinity (linked to nationality) wherever it is played, although there are differing levels of this as seen in Chapter 3 in the case of the differences between full and associate member countries.

In Chapter 2 of this book, the relationship between cricket and masculinity was traced through exploring the dual process of parliamentarisation and sportisation in English cricket, and it is argued that these two processes are distinctly gendered. Sportisation has not always been discussed as a gendered process, but given the time in which the sportisation of cricket occurred the gendered nature of this is significant and can be understood as the emergence of specific and distinct established and outsider relations with extensive power differentiation. It is also evident, through considering the diffusion of cricket (which arguably is not linear or straightforward), that cricket was diffused as a male sport that came to represent types of nationality (and national identity) and masculinity in varying contexts. This occurred alongside the emergence of established and outsider figurations which enabled male cricketers, both nationally and internationally, to control the physicality, ideologies and organisational networks associated with the game. However it is important to stress here that in all the cases discussed in this book and in all countries in which the women's game is played, it is not the objective or subjective nature of knowledge that defines cricket as masculine, but rather social processes that enable and perpetuate social inequalities in the game to continue.

Through examining long-term social processes from the emergence of the women's game to the present structure and global governance of the game, it is evident that there has been a clear civilising trend alongside a broader reduction of power relations between male and female cricketers, both globally and within nation states. The tracing of long-term social processes is critical in this regard to prevent what Elias termed the tendency of sociologists to retreat to the present. When examining the emergence and development of women's cricket, it is important to recognise that women's cricket is now a visible, albeit marginal, part of the global game. In this regard, a process of functional democratisation has taken place which ensures that women have far greater opportunities within this established and outsider figuration, which is arguably in flux with complex shifting mutual power balances. This change in power relations is not self-contained but is reflected in broader changes as noted, for example, in changes in economic structures of society, education level of women, role of law in ensuring women's rights, women's greater entry in public spheres and broader changes in relation to manners and standards of emotional control among men and women, which require higher demands on people's capacity for self-regulation and restraint.

Functional democratisation and continuing power relations between men's and women's cricket

In identifying a shift of power between men and women in the women's game, I am not suggesting that power relations between men and women have completely equalised. There are numerous examples throughout this book where it is evident that there remain power imbalances between men and women cricketers that continue to position men's cricket as the established group. Some examples include how male cricketers continue to monopolise key resources, although women are starting to gain access through organisational changes. Alongside these organisational changes, there is greater mutual identification and negotiation about these resources, but ultimately it is the International Cricket Council (ICC) and other national gender-integrated organisations, often dominated by men, that decide on how resources are shared. Women cricketers are now part of the organisational networks such as national governing bodies and the international governing body such as the ICC that decide on how resources are shared, although their role within these organisational networks, nationally and internationally, can be marginal. Long-term social processes suggest that there are changing mutual power balances whereby women have gradually utilised power resources to position themselves as outsiders within these networks as opposed to being separate from these.

These processes are by no means linear nor are they monodirectional (Brinkgreve, 2004). Women may have access to greater power resources through two key forums:, firstly in that they give global organisations access to greater financial gains (giving women a function in the men's game) through greater ability to access funds, but also to demonstrate 'gender equity' within global organisations; and secondly for organisations to be seen as 'morally responsible' in supporting all people to participate in cricket. These power resources may be fragile and may also be at times 'front facing' in that the actions behind the rhetoric of gender equity in national and global sporting governance are not entirely clear or upfront or can mask much more deep-seated social habituses and attitudes that continue to consider women cricketers as outsiders.

Women and men who play cricket, alongside those involved in the governance of the game, have greater density of interdependency than in previous years and contexts. This means they are more aware of one another. Male cricketing associations now have to consider the ambitions and feelings of women and women cricketers as well as demonstrating, on paper at least, that they are committed to developing a strategy to ensure that the global game develops. As Mansfield (2008: 95) highlights, there is an

> inextricable relationship between social development (sociogenesis) and developments in personality structures (psychogenesis) and power relations in terms of tensions between established and outsider groups.

Women are represented but not necessarily on the boards of national and international organisations of the game. Nevertheless these organisations represent the women's game and these changes however have resulted in a shift in the psychogenesis of both groups in which men are more willing to accept that women should have opportunities to play the game. Despite this the relations between the two groups remain unequal with the women's game having less access to financial rewards to enable them power within national and global organisations; thus the women appear part of global organisations but in many respects the established group has greater access to be able to control and benefit from the success of the women's game.

Consideration of monopoly of physicality, ideology and organisational networks in gender relations

In analysing the long-term developments in the game, men's monopolisation of physicality, ideology (knowledge) and organisational networks has reduced. Within these relations it is important to recognise that tensions and power balances still exist, that the women's game is not as advanced or as supported as the men's game and that the amount of resources in the two sports continues to be unbalanced. One example of the continual monopoly of ideological (knowledge) networks is that the term cricket is still seen to represent men's cricket. For example, the ICC Cricket World Cup automatically means the men's World Cup, whereas women's cricket is always demarcated by the term 'women'. For example, it is the ICC Women's World Cup. Thus cricket has come to mean men's cricket. A similar trend is found on the websites of the national governing bodies, in which, for example, England news is different from the section on the England women's cricket team. The ideological association of 'cricket' as a male sport is widely accepted whereas women's cricket demarcates a different (inferior) form of cricket.

Physical strength in sport and discussions about cricket are also something that continue to be referenced in relation to men's and women's cricketing bodies. For example, in the introduction to this book, I drew on media reports about Sarah Taylor and discussions about her competing in men's cricket. These discussions centre predominantly on whether she has the physical strength *in comparison to male cricketers*. These discussions focus on the physical body, which is embodied with social power dynamics that continue to position men as more suitable for sport. Men's bodies are presented as stronger and faster, which makes the men's game more exciting; thus one consequence of greater interdependence is that comparisons between the established and the outsider groups' ability to play the game may enable the established group to draw more on seemingly unchanging factors, such as biology – which is presented as natural, fixed and unchangeable – as a reason for their continual established status, as well as justifying a kind of 'inequality that has been codified . . . in such a way it became not only custom but habit' (Elias, 1987: 287). In cricket, a move towards faster versions of the game, for example, T20 one-day internationals and the Indian Premier League, have shifted cricket in some respects to rely more on strength and speed than previous versions of the game. This emphasis on these forms of the game arguably enable more direct comparison that may favour the established group and give them examples to prove that they are physically superior and that the men's game is more exciting and thus more marketable and commercial than the women's game. However it is important to note that through greater levels of dependency, there is less opportunity for one individual to control the outcomes, and in larger global organisations, it could be argued that 'chains of interdependence become differentiated and grow denser; consequently they become more opaque and, for any single group or individual, more uncontrollable' (Elias, 1978: 68). In a recent article, the *Telegraph* discussed the new contracts given to England women, drawing a direct comparison:

> They may be doing better than the men but they are very different animals. First there is the question of physicality. The men's cricket ball weighs 5.5oz, the women's five. A Test match is played over four days, not five. The boundary is brought in for women. They cannot bowl as fast – the top speed of about 75mph is 15mph slower than the fastest men. They cannot throw as far (although, while several years ago there was perhaps only one woman on the team who could throw in direct from the boundary, nowadays there are four or five). And they cannot hit as hard.

Another consequence of greater interdependence means that the women are now more dependent on the established group, thus in terms of strategic development of the game, funding, ideological support of women playing and so on are now decided by an organisation that claims to represent both male and female cricketers, but in reality the mergers between the International Women's Cricket Council (IWCC) and the ICC and those at national levels required the women's organisations to merge. Yet as Stronach and Adair (2009) suggest in their analysis of the Australian context, these mergers can look more like takeovers than mergers as integration is not easily evidenced in these case studies. One of the reasons for this may be that the men's organisations change very little in these mergers, so, whilst women's organisations disband, the men's organisations do not change their structure to accommodate the women's game and are not impacted on a day-to-day basis by the involvement of women.

In these case studies, as discussed in Chapter 4, the women's game becomes integrated into an organisation that previously had not been involved in the women's game, in many respects women go into this process as the weaker partners (as their organisations were failing due to lack of funds). In many cases, the mergers were driven by lack of finances on behalf of the women's game, so their ability to influence and shape decisions made within this larger organisation is yet to be seen, but in many ways this merger ties them closer to the established group. Theoretically speaking, this gives women greater power within the figuration, but it also makes them dependent on an organisation they may feel they have little power to be able to control, see, for example, Chapter 5 and the issues relating to the merger of the England Women's Cricket Association (EWCA) and the England and Wales Cricket Board (ECB). Women are unable to reverse the decision to merge and reestablish their own organisational networks, despite concerns raised about this organisational merging and their lack of control over how the game should develop.

In these cases, it could be seen that through mergers, the established have gained greater control over the development of the women's game. In doing so, the established group has increasing opportunities to be involved in positions of power in the women's game, i.e. coaching of national teams and controlling the strategy for the development of the women's game. Women who speak out against such changes may be seen as radicals who do not appreciate the support and improved benefits that the women's game has received from the merger and the increased support from the established male group. As an outsider group, through the history of the development of women's cricket, women have been conscious of the views of the established group, careful not to offend, keen not to be seen as demanding of the established group and largely keen to be seen as internalising their group disgrace (i.e. accepting that the women's game is inferior to the men's game). Thus many female cricketers continue to accept their outsider status, understand why the established group should have better access to resources, facilities, commercialisation and sponsorship as they agree that it is part of the more dominant form of the game.

In theory the increased dependency between the two groups should also facilitate a change in male habituses in which male preserves begin to change. This is something for another study, but other than the organisational networks that have enabled greater mutual identification between the men's and women's games, this shift is less clearly seen in men's cricket. Instead the desire to continue to monopolise resources (albeit by different means than violence or ignoring the outsider group) giving up monopolisation of resources is not easy for the established group. In short I would argue that relations between male and female cricketers are no less constraining in these new figurations but are increasingly complex and determined by complex fragmented established and outsider groups, and it is to the use of established and outsider relations as a framework for the analysis of gender relations I now turn.

The theory of established and outsider relations cannot be considered as separate from Eliasian concepts more broadly, that is civilising processes must be considered as part of a figurational analysis more. In considering the emergence of established and outsider relations and the changing power relations between two groups, it is worth considering how adequate the framework is for such an analysis. Liston (2014) has recently noted in her use of the theory of established and outsider to study gender relations that it 'seems to create different kinds of resistance, from patronizing dismissals of women's sport to heightening of resentment' (2014). In this regard, in the shifting power balances between the sexes and in figurations where greater interdependency is a reality, perhaps more needs to be considered about how the outsider group internalises its outsider status in these increasing interdependencies to which it is tied. Like Liston (2014), I would suggest more needs to be considered about the fragmentation of both established and outsider groups. For example, female cricket fans who continue to support male teams across the globe may not be complimentary about the women's game and may not be interested in supporting women's cricket. Furthermore, some women accept the established view that the women's game is inferior; however, some members of the established male group are supportive of the women's game, in particular fathers, brothers and male coaches may play an integral role in developing female cricketers both personally but also organisationally and some males support the women's game extensively. This clearly demonstrates a mix of identities that the established group has. However, the question needs to be posed as to under what conditions does the established group begin to identify more with the outsider group. This may relate to increased mutual identification; as Messner (2005) suggests, the role of significant males who support women may be the result of increased mutual identification with a female group, thus making them more empathetic to listen and negotiate to the needs of a specific group. Appointing male coaches may seem to be contrary to the development of women's sport by denying women these positions of relative power (especially in regard to ideology). Taking a long-term approach may enable a more detached perspective to consider how the mutual identification with females and female cricketers may enable these males, who are within the established group, to further question and challenge the established group to allow more opportunities for outsiders within the cricket figuration (although this remains to be seen). These ideas need greater theoretical consideration in developing the theory of established and outsider relations. Thus within established and outsider groups there are 'outsiders within'; this is a 'function of the degree of social cohesiveness within a group' (Liston, 2014: 212). Some members of the established group identify more with the outsider group, but this aspect of established and outsider remains undertheorised.

Out of all of Elias' concepts, the theory of established and outsider relations has received the least critical review, yet from figurational sociologists there have been some concerns raised about the concept as a framework for the analysis of power relations. For example, Bloyce and Murphy (2007) offer a detailed critique of established and outsider relations as a seemingly binary model, suggesting the framework might be more applicable in contexts when the two groups are relatively detached from wider human figurations. I agree that the terms 'established' and 'outsider' seem at odds with the fluidity of other terminology in figurational sociology (Malcolm, 2014). However, I would suggest that the theory focus on the relationship and networks of interdependency and power relations between (and therefore social processes) and also within the two groups, that is, the fragmentation of relations, networks and interdependencies between groups. Thus within established and outsider groups, there are notable outsider groups and complex figurations between established and outsider groups. Thus whilst the language of established and outsider might appear binary, it is possible through looking at the social processes that enable the established and outsiders to maintain their positions within the figuration through phases of functional democratisation how such relations influence social habituses within groups. Furthermore it is important to consider how the relations between established and outsider groups are fragmented and far from binary.

In considering civilising processes, civilising directions can also be reversed or can become more stabilised, and based on the relationship between the sexes, power balances between the two groups could affect the habituses of both groups. This may increase equalisation of the two groups or it may enable the established group to control the social habituses of the outsider group in ways that continue to position the outsiders as outsiders in the cricket figuration. The theory of established and outsider relations is useful for considering not the truth or reality of established and outsider groups but for considering the 'social conditions in which knowledge is generated and developed through application' (Malcolm, 2014: 8) and how power relations can be both enabling and constraining in such figurations. In the emergence and development of women's cricket, the conditions in which knowledge has been generated in established and outsider relations, with relatively extensive power relations to those where these relations are in flux, are critical to how social processes and continual struggles play out in the women's game. In tracing long-term social processes, it is possible to prevent what Elias termed the tendency of sociologists to retreat to the present to consider how the game developed in particular ways that enabled the first international match to be played between Australia and England in 1934.

Women's cricket as 'a global game'

Women's cricket is a global sport; it is governed by a global organisation, the ICC. The women's game has developed in several of the full membership countries (and increasingly outside of these), although support within different nations is varying, as Chapter 3 highlights. Women's cricket continues to face difficulties in developing recognition, sponsorship, commercial developments and spectatorship. Many women cricketers are in a position of playing a professional game but are amateur or at least cannot afford to concentrate on playing the game as a means of livelihood. In part the relationship between cricket, masculinity and the nation globally has meant that ideologically the women's game does not invoke in people a sense of national pride; whether women win or lose the game can be ignored by media accounts that continue to privilege male cricketers. The emergence of the state was gendered (although little is written about this) and the dual roles of sportisation and parliamentarisation processes were also clearly gendered (although again little is discussed about this in wider literature).

In relation to the pattern of development in cricket, there are some noticeable differences between the men's and women's games, especially the role of minority cricketing countries, such as Holland and Ireland and their roles in the IWCC, before more established cricketing countries such as Sri Lanka and Pakistan who did not emerge on the international scene until much later. The IWCC as an organisation was far less influential in the development of the game than the male governing body in men's cricket, partially a consequence of being an outsider group. The IWCC was governed predominantly by the national governing bodies, and as these were struggling to develop both financially and ideologically, the IWCC struggled to govern the game or lead in its development. Financially insecure and lacking international recognition, the organisation struggled with governance and strategic development, lacking power in being able to shape the development of the global game and in the end was forced to merge with the ICC, which led to broader changes in the women's game.

Current changes in women's cricket seem to be quite fast paced and it could be argued the game is going through a stage of emancipation and is a challenge to existing established and outsider figurations. For example in May 2014, as I was finishing writing this book, it was announced that a premier league-style tournament for women could be developed within the next year. The Women's International Cricket League is being proposed by an Australian businessman. This would the first commercially driven enterprise of the women's game, interestingly not one developed by the ICC. The proposal is to bring the best female players in the world to play with and against each other in 6 company-owned teams over a 12-day event to be held in Singapore. This would signal a shift in the women's game, as it would be the first standalone commercial development of the women's game, with women becoming able to make money from playing in such a tournament funded by companies and sponsorship (Mitchell, 2014). Discussions around the tournament have focused on issues not often discussed in the women's game, such as match fixing which has been an ongoing issue in men's cricket. The idea of such a proposal demonstrates a clear shift in the women's game as few commercial women's leagues exist in any team sport.

In *Women's Cricket and Global Processes: The Emergence and Development of Women's Cricket as a Global Game'*, I have focused on gender relations and not discussed extensively racial, sexualised or class aspects of the women's game. These issues may need to be considered further as the global game develops and, within the game, racial and class tensions are played out more prominently than in the global game. Little is written about racism in women's cricket or little is reported on it; however it is important to consider that issues of race and racism have impacted on the emergence of the women's game, yet this aspect of the game remains little discussed. Similarly there is little discussion about homophobia in the women's game as the women's game presents a united front to develop the game as a cohesive outsider group; at times these issues have remained under-researched and underdiscussed. Few governing bodies have a policy with regard to issues of power, sexuality and race in women's sport, and in men's cricket, issues of race and racism have received academic discussion and high-profile cases have demonstrated tensions around race relations and racism in the men's game. Little is understood about these issues in the women's game.

The experience of outsider groups, like established groups, are of course divided by notions of difference and competing views of masculinity and femininity are produced and reproduced through media imagery. This may need broader discussion in the context of the established male group where traditional views of masculinity and the nation are inextricably linked to heterosexuality at present, but this may become more destabilised as more sportsmen identify as homosexual. At present, few elite male cricketers have identified as homosexual and therefore the dominant notion of the heterosexual masculine cricketers is a dominant discourse of the global men's game.

Another consideration is media sport networks and the role they play in defining and reinforcing ideas about outsider groups. As the women's game develops, and images of the game are transmitted and discussed, the role of the media–sport nexus in global sport has to date not wholly impacted on women's cricket, women's cricket and discussions in the media often draw on comparisons to the men's game. The role of the media and sponsorship and any commercial leagues and their success will be of interest to consider in future analyses of the women's game. Women's cricket is shown on television in different national contexts and in international tournaments but the production of these matches can somewhat lack the glamour and soap opera drama of men's cricket. The media are therefore constructing images about women and cricket that needs further analysis moving forward.

The 2009 World Cup was the first tournament to receive global televised coverage and the extent to which the women's game can evoke feelings of national identity and pride is yet to be seen. The women's game does not represent such strong notions of nation and this may reflect one of the continuing consequences of being an outsider group in an established and outsider figuration. Further analysis of women's sport needs to consider the complexity of long-term social processes that have enabled women's sport to develop, by considering power relations and power imbalances both between established and outsider groups and also between outsider groups. Further analysis may need to consider the ongoing constraining aspects of an established and outsider figuration that continue to position women as outsiders in the global cricket figuration more broadly. It is hoped this book goes some way to understanding these issues and applying the theory to understanding the emergence and development of women's cricket as a global game.

References

Allen, D. (2010). South African Cricket and British Imperialism, 1870–1910. *The Changing Face of Cricket: From Imperial to Global Game*, D. Malcolm, J. Gemmell and N. Nehta (eds). London: Routledge, 34–51.

Appadurai, A. (1996). *Modernity at Large: Cultural Dimensions Globalization.* Minneapolis: University of Minnesota Press.

Archdale, B. (1937). The Australian Players. *Women's Cricket.* Knebworth, UK: Pollard Publications, vol. 8, p. 6.

Bairner, A. (2001). *Sport, Nationalism, and Globalization: European and North American Perspectives.* New York: SUNY Press.

Bandyopadhyay, K. (2007). Pakistani Cricket at Crossroads: An Outsider's Perspective. *Sport in Society* 10(1): 101.

BBC Sport (2014). England Women Earn 18 New Central Contracts. Retrieved 7 August 2014, from http://www.bbc.co.uk/sport/0/cricket/27291212

Beckles, H. (1998). *The Development of West Indies Cricket, Vol 1: The Age of Nationalism.* Jamaica: The Press University of the West Indies.

Benn, T. and B. Benn (2004). After Olga: Developments in Women's Artistic Gymnastics Following the 1972 'Olga Korbut phenomenon'. *Sport Histories: Figurational Studies of the Development of Modern Sports.* E. Dunning, D. Malcolm and I. Waddington (eds). London: Routledge, 172–191.

Bloyce, D. and P. Murphy (2007). Involvement and Detachment, from Principles to Practice: A Critical Reassessment of the Established and the Outsiders. *Irish Journal of Sociology* 16(1): 3–21.

Bose, M. (2006). *The Magic of Indian Cricket: Cricket and Society in India.* London: Routledge.

Botelho, V. L. and S. Agergaard (2011). Moving for the Love of the Game? International Migration of Female Footballers into Scandinavian Countries. *Soccer & Society* 12(6): 806.

Brinkgreve, C. (2003). On Modern Relationships: The Commandments of the New Freedom. *Norbert Elias.* E. Dunning and N. Elias (eds). London: Sage Publishers, 251–260.

Brinkgreve, C. (2004). Elias and Gender Relations: The Changing Balance of Power between the Sexes. *The Sociology of Norbert Elias.* S. Loyal and S. Quilley (eds). Cambridge: Cambridge University Press.

Brookes, C. (1978). *English Cricket: The Game and It's Players through the Ages.* London: Weidenfeld & Nicholson.

Butcher, B. (1996). *Ice-Cream with Chilli Powder: A Manager's Account of a Women's Cricket Tour of India in the 1970's.* Victoria, Australia: Print Synergy Pty Ltd.

Cashman, R. (1998). Australia. *The Imperial Game.* B. Stoddart and K. Sandiford (eds). Manchester: Manchester University Press, 34–53.

Cashman, R. and R. Weaver (1991). *Wicket Women: Cricket and Women in Australia*. Australia: New South Wales University Press.

Cooper, I. (2004). Game, Set and Match: Lawn Tennis, from Early Origins to Modern Sport. *Sport Histories: Figurational Studies of the Development of Modern Sports*. E. Dunning, D. Malcolm and I. Waddington (eds). London: Routledge, 104–121.

Duncan, I. (2013). *Skirting the Boundary: A History of Women's Cricket*. London: The Robson Press.

Dunning, E. (1999). *Sport Matters: Sociological Studies of Sport, Violence and Civilization*. London: Routledge.

Dunning, E. and J. Hughes (2013). *Norbert Elias and Modern Sociology: Knowledge, Interdependence, Power, Process*. London: Bloomsbury.

Elias, N. (1978). *What is Sociology?* Columbia: Columbia University Press.

Elias, N. (1987). The Changing Balance of Power between the Sexes in Ancient Rome. *Theory, Culture and Society* 4(2–3): 287–316.

Elias, N. (2000). *The Civilising Process*. London: Wiley Blackwell.

Elias, E. and E. Dunning (1986). *Quest for Excitement Sport and Leisure in the Civilizing Process*. Oxford: Blackwell.

Elliott, R. and J. Maguire (2008). Thinking Outside of the Box: Exploring a Conceptual Synthesis for Research in the Area of Athletic Labor Migration. *Sociology of Sport Journal* 25(4): 482–497.

Elias, N. and J. Scotson (1994). *The Established and the Outsiders*. London: Sage Publications.

Gemmell, J. (2004). *The Politics of South African Cricket*. London: Routledge.

Gleadle, K. (2009). *Borderline Citizens: Women, Gender and Political Culture in Britain 1815–1867*. Oxford: Oxford University Press.

Gupta, R. (2013). Bowled Out of the Game: Nationalism and Gender Equality in Indian Cricket. *Berkeley Journal of Entertainment and Sports Law* 2(1): 90–119.

Guttmann, A. (1991). *Women's Sports: A History*. New York: Columbia University Press.

Hamid, T. (1978). Subject: Pakistan Women's Cricket Association. Retrieved 22 November 2012, from http://static.espncricinfo.com/db/NATIONAL/PAK/ASSOCIATIONS/PWCA/ARCHIVE/Transcript-1-1978.htm

Hamid, T. (1979). Ref. No. PWCA/1/79. Retrieved 22 November 2012, from http://static.espncricinfo.com/db/NATIONAL/PAK/ASSOCIATIONS/PWCA/ARCHIVE/Transcript-6-1979.html

Hargreaves, J. (1992). Sex, Gender and the Civilising Process: Has there been a Civilising Process? *Sport and Leisure in the Civilising Process: Critique and Counter Critique*. E. Dunning and C. Rojek (eds). Toronto: University of Toronto Press, 161–182.

Hargreaves, J. (1994). *Sporting Females: Critical Issues in the History and Sociology of Women's Sports*. London: Routledge.

Harris, C. (1997). Changing Times Ahead. *Wicket Women*. Summer.

Heinrich, S. (2004). ICC Saves Women's World Cup. 27 June. Retrieved 11 August 2014, from http://news.bbc.co.uk/sport1/hi/cricket/3844103.stm

Heyhoe Flint, R. (1978). *Heyhoe! The Autobiography of Rachael Heyhoe Flint*. London: Pelham Books.

Heyhoe Flint, R. and N. Rheinberg (1976). *Fair Play: The Story of Women's Cricket*. London: Angus and Robertson.

Hoeber, L. (2007). Exploring the Gaps between Meanings and Practices of Gender Equity in a Sport Organization. *Gender, Work and Organization* 14(3): 259–280.

Hussain, J. (2013). Leading Women's Cricket in Pakistan. Retrieved 23 April 2014, from http://www.youlinmagazine.com/article/leading-women-cricket-in-pakistan/MTUw

Hutton Whitelaw, M. (1936). *Cricket in New Zealand*. Women's Cricket, vol. 7, no. 2. Knebworth: Pollard Publications.

Jan, F. (2010). Pakistan: A Struggling Nation-State. *Democracy and Security* 6: 237–255.

Jarvie, G. and J. Maguire (2004). *Sport and Leisure in Social Thought*. London: Routledge.

Joy, N. (1950). *Maiden Over: A Short History of Women's Cricket and a Report of the Australian Tour 1948–49*. London: Sporting Handbooks Limited.

Khan, S. and A. Khan (2013). *Cricket Cauldron: The Turbulent Politics of Sport in Pakistan*. London: I. B. Tauris.

Lake, R. (2009). Real Tennis and Civilising Processes. *Sport in History* 29(4): 553–576.

Liston, K. (2005). Established-Outsider Relations between Males and Females in Male-Associated Sports in Ireland. *European Journal for Sport and Society* 2(1): 25–33.

Liston, K. (2006). Women's Soccer in the Republic of Ireland: Some Preliminary Sociological Comments. *Soccer and Society* 7(2): 364–384.

Liston, K. (2014). Revisiting Relations between the Sexes in Sport on the Island of Ireland. In *Norbert Elias and Empirical Research*. F. Dépelteau and T. S. Landini (eds). New York: Palgrave Macmillan, 197–219.

Liston, K. and E. Moreland (2009). Hockey and Habitus: Sport and National Identity in Northern Ireland. *New Hibernia Review* 13(4): 127–140.

Little, C. (2012). 'Despicable and Degrading': Australian-Ceylonese Sporting Relations. *Sport in Society: Cultures, Commerce, Media, Politics* 15(4): 428–446.

Maguire, J. (1993). Globalization, Sport and National Identities: The Empires Strike Back? (Globalisation, sport et identite nationale: les empires contre-attaquent-ils?). *Society & Leisure/Loisir & Société* 16(2): 293–321.

Maguire, J. (1999). *Global Sport: Identities, Societies, Civilizations*. Cambridge: Polity Press.

Maguire, J. (2005). Introduction. *Power and Global Sport: Zones of Prestige, Emulation and Resistance*. J. Maguire (ed.). London: Routledge, 1–21.

Maguire, J. (2011). Sport, Identity Politics, Gender and Globalization. *Sport in Society* 14(7/8): 994–1009.

Maguire, J. (2012). *Reflections on Process Sociology and Sport: 'Walking the Line'*. London: Routledge.

Maguire, J. and L. Mansfield (1998). No-Body's Perfect: Women, Aerobics and the Body Beautiful. *Sociology of Sport Journal* 15(2): 109–137.

Majumdar, B. (2003). Cricket in Colonial India: The Bombay Pentangular, 1892–1946. *Sport in Asian Society: Past and Present.* J. A. Mangan and F. Hong (eds). London: Frank Cass, 157–189.

Majumdar, B. and J. A. Mangan (2004). *Cricketing Cultures in Conflict: World Cup 2003.* London: Routledge.

Malcolm, D. (2001). 'It's not Cricket': Colonial Legacies and Contemporary Inequalities. *Journal of Historical Sociology* 14(3): 253.

Malcolm, D. (2002). Cricket and Civilising Processes. *International Review for the Sociology of Sport* 37(1): 37–57.

Malcolm, D. (2004). Cricket: Civilizing and De-civilising Processes in the Imperial Game. *Sport Histories: Figurational Studies of the Development of Modern Sports.* E. Dunning, D. Malcolm and I. Waddington (eds). London: Routledge, 71–88.

Malcolm, D. (2005). The Emergence, Codification and Diffusion of Sport: Theoretical and Conceptual Issues. *International Review for the Sociology of Sport* 40(1): 115–118.

Malcolm, D. (2012). *Sport and Sociology.* London: Routledge.

Malcolm, D. (2013). *Globalizing Cricket: Englishness, Empire and Identity.* London: Bloomsbury.

Malcolm, D. and P. Velija (2008). Female Incursions into Cricket's Male Preserve. *Tribal Play: Subcultural Journeys through Sport.* M. Aitkinson and K. Young (eds). Bingley, UK: Emerald Group, 217–235.

Malcolm, D., J. Gemmell, and N. Mehta (2009). Cricket and Modernity: International and Interdisciplinary Perspectives on the Study of the Imperial Game. *Sport in Society* 12: 431–446.

Mandle, W. F. (1973). Cricket and Australian Nationalism in the Nineteenth Century. *Journal of the Royal Australian Historical Society*, 59(4): 225–246.

Mangan, J. A. (2010). Imperial Origins: Christian Manliness, Moral Imperatives and Pre-Sri Lankan Playing Fields. *The International Journal of the History of Sport* 27(1–2): 424–469.

Mansfield, L. (2002). Feminist and Figurational Sociology. *Research in the Sociology of Sport: Theory, Sport and Society.* J. Maguire and K. Young (eds). London: Reed Elsevier Science, 317–335.

Mansfield, L. (2008). Reconsidering Feminism and the Work of Norbert Elias for Understanding Gender, Sport and Sport-Related Activities. *European Physical Education Review* 14(1): 93–121.

Mansfield, L. (2010). Fit, Fat and Feminine: The Stigmatisation of Fat Women in Fitness Gyms. *Women and Exercise: Qualitative Research on the Body, Health and Consumerism.* E. Kennedy and P. Markula (eds). London: Routledge, 81–101.

Mansfield, L. and H. Curtis (2009). Competing Women: Media Representations of Femininity and National Identification at the Olympic Games in Athens in 2004. *Esporte e Sociedade* 4(12): 1–26.

Marjoribanks, T. and K. Farquharson (2012). *Sport and Society in the Global Age.* Basingstoke: Palgrave Macmillan.

McCrone, K. (1988). *Sport and the Physical Emancipation of English Women 1870–1914*. London: Routledge.

McRae, D. (2013). England Cricketer Sarah Taylor Could Make History in Men's County Match. *The Guardian*. Retrieved 15 January 2013, from http://www.guardian.co.uk/sport/2013/jan/14/england-cricketer-sarah-taylor-mens-match

Mennell, S. (1992). *Norbert Elias: An Introduction*. Dublin: University College Dublin Press.

Messner, M. (2005). *Taking the Field: Women, Men and Sports*. Minnesota: Minnesota Press.

Mierzwinski, M., P. Velija and D. Malcolm (2014). Women's Experiences in the Mixed Martial Arts: A Quest for Excitement? *Sociology of Sport Journal* 31: 66–84.

Mitchell, A. (2014). Women's Twenty20: New IPL-Style League Planned by Australian Pair. BBC Sport.

Morrison, L. (1993). The AIAW: Governance by Women for Women. *Women in Sport: Issues and Controversies*. G.L. Cohen (ed). London: Sage Publications, 59–66.

Mustafa, F. (2013). Cricket and Globalization: Global Processes and the Imperial Game. *Journal of Global History* 8: 318–341.

Naha, D. (2012). Adams and Eves at the Eden Gardens: Women and Cricket Spectators and the Conflict of Feminine Subjectivity in Calcutta, 1920–1970. *The International Journal of the History of Sport* 29(5): 711–729.

Nasim, R. (1980). Retrieved 22 November 2012, from http://static.espncricinfo.com/db/NATIONAL/PAK/ASSOCIATIONS/PWCA/ARCHIVE/Transcript-3-1980.html

Nauright, J. (2010). *Long Run to Freedom: Sport, Cultures and Identities in South Africa*. Morgantown, WV: Fitness Information Technology.

Odendaal, A. (2011). 'Neither Cricketers nor Ladies': Towards a History of Women and Cricket in South Africa, 1860's–2000. *The International Journal of the History of Sport* 28(1): 115–136.

Paolucci, T. (2010). Vigoro Championships to be Played on Strathfieldsaye's Fields. *Bendigo Advertiser*. Bendigo.

Parry, M. and Malcolm, D. (2004). England's Barmy Army. *Commercialization, Masculinity and Nationalism* 39(1): 75–94.

Perera, S. (2000). 'Cricket with a Plot': Nationalism, Cricket and Diasporic Identities. *Journal of Australian Studies* 65: 22.

Pollard, M. (1933). *Cricket for Women and Girls*. England: Hutchinson.

Pope, S. (2011). 'Like Pulling Down Durham Cathedral and Building a Brothel': Women as 'New Consumer' Fans? *International Review for the Sociology of Sport* 46(4): 471–487.

PWCA (1980). Subject: Pakistan Women Cricket Team. Retrieved 7 June 2013, from http://static.espncricinfo.com/db/NATIONAL/PAK/ASSOCIATIONS/PWCA/ARCHIVE/Transcript-3-1980.html

PWCA (1981). Sub: Affiliation of Pakistan Women Cricket Association with BCCP. Retrieved 7 June 2013, from http://static.espncricinfo.com/db/NATIONAL/PAK/ASSOCIATIONS/PWCA/ARCHIVE/Transcript-4-1981.html

Quilley, S. and S. Loyal (2005). Eliasian Sociology as a 'Central Theory' for the Social Sciences. *Current Sociology* 53(5): 807–828.

Raj, A. and L. McDougal (2014). Sexual Violence and Rape in India. *The Lancet* 383(9920): 865.

Roberts, M. (2006). *Essaying Cricket: Sri Lanka and Beyond*. Colombo: Vijitha Yapa Publishers.

Roberts, M. (2010). Wunderkidz in a Blunderland: Tensions and Tales from Sri Lankan Cricket. *The Changing Face of Cricket: From Imperial to Global Game*. D. Malcolm, J. Gemmell and N. Mehta (eds). London: Routledge, 136–149.

Ryan, G. (2004). *The Making of New Zealand Cricket 1832–1914*. London: Frank Cass.

Sandiford, K. (1998). The Imperial Game: England. *The Imperial Game*. B. Stoddart and K. Sandiford (eds). Manchester: Manchester University Press, 9–34.

Shaw, S. and T. Slack (2002). 'It's been like that for Donkey's Years': The Construction of Gender Relations and the Cultures of Sports Organizations. *Culture, Sport, Society* 5(1): 86–106.

Sheard, K. (2004). Boxing in the Western Civilising Process. *Sport Histories Figurational Studies of the Development of Modern Sport*. E. Dunning, D. Malcolm and I. Waddington (eds). Oxon: Routledge, 15–31.

Shemilt, S. (2014). Women's Ashes: Men's Whitewash Gives England 'Extra Spur'. Retrieved 13 January 2014, from http://www.bbc.co.uk/sport/0/cricket/25627152

Skillen, F. (2012). 'It's Possible to Play the Game Marvelously and at the Same Time Look Pretty and Be Perfectly Fit': Sport, Women and Fashion in Interwar Britain. *Costume* 46(2): 165–180.

Steen, R. (2010). Acronym Wars: The Economics and Indianisation of Contemporary Cricket. *Cricket and Globalization*. C. Rumford and S. Wagg (eds). Newcastle: Cambridge Scholars Publishing, 84.

Stevenson, D. (2002). Women, Sport and Globalization: Competing Discourses of Sexuality and Nation. *Journal of Sport and Social Issues* 26: 209–225.

Stronach, M. and D. Adair (2009). 'Brave New World' or 'Sticky Wicket'? Women, Management and Organizational Power in Cricket Australia. *Sport in Society* 12(1): 910–932.

Thadani, K., S. Sharma and D. Chakravarti (2012). *Women and Sport in India and the World*. Saarbruken, Germany: Lambert Academic.

Thing, L. F. (2001). The Female Warrior: Meanings of Play-Aggressive Emotions in Sport. *International Review for the Sociology of Sport* 36(3): 275–288.

Thompson, S. (1990). 'Thank the Ladies for the Plates': The Incorporation of Women into Sport. *Leisure Studies* 9: 135–143.

Treibel, A. (2001). The Changing Balance of Power between Men and Women: A Figurational Study of the Public and Private Spheres in Western Societies. *Norbert Elias and Human Interdependencies*. T. Salumets (ed.). London: McGill-Queen's University Press, 175–190.

Twitchen, A. (2004). The Influence of State Formation Processes on the Early Development of Motor Racing. *Sport Histories: Figurational Studies of the Development of Modern Sports*. E. Dunning, D. Malcolm and I. Waddington (eds). London: Routledge, 121–137.

UK Sports Council (2004). Women and Sport: From Brighton to Windhoek Facing the Challenge. International Working Group on Women and Sport (IWG), http://www.sportanddev.org/newsnviews/search.cfm?uNewsID=55

Valiotis, C. (2009). Runs in the Outfield: The Pakistani Diaspora and Cricket in England. *International Journal of the History of Sport* 26(12): 1791–1822.

Van Stolk, B. and C. Wouters (1987). Power Changes and Self Respect: A Comparison of Two Cases of Established-Outsider Relations. *Theory, Culture and Society* 4: 477–488.

Velija, P., A. Ratna, and A. Flintoff (2010). Women at the Wicket: The Development of Women's Cricket. *Cricket and Globalization*. C. Rumford and S. Wagg (eds). Newcastle Upon Tyne: Cambridge Scholars Publishing, 103–122.

WCA (Women's Cricket Association) (1926). Women's Cricket Association: Minutes of 1st Meeting, 1–3.

WCA (Women's Cricket Association) (1927). Report, 1927, Women's Cricket Association Birmingham: WCA, 1–13.

WCA (Women's Cricket Association) (1972). Women's Cricket Association Year Book 1972. *Year Book*. Birmingham: WCA.

WCA (Women's Cricket Association) (1986). Women's Cricket and the Women's Cricket Association Today. *WCA News Winter 1986*, 1.

Werbner, P. (1996). 'Our Blood is Green': Cricket, Identity and Social Empowerment among British Pakistanis. *Sport, Identity and Ethnicity*. J. MacClancy (ed.). Oxford: Berg, 69–87.

Whitehorn, N. (1956). International Women's Cricket Council. *Women's Cricket Association Report 1956*: 68.

Williams, J. (2001). *Cricket and Race*. Oxford: Berg.

Williamson, L. (2012). 'After Twenty20 World Cup we must now start taking women's cricket seriously'. Mail online, 7 October 2012, accessed 26 January 2014, http://www.dailymail.co.uk/sport/article-2214296/We-start-taking-womens-cricket-seriously--Laura-Williamson.html

Wolfe, J. (1991). The Global and the Specific: Reconciling Conflicting Theories of Culture. *Culture, Globalization and the World-System*. A. D. King (ed.). Macmillan: London, 161–173.

Women's Cricket Association (1930). WCA Official Organ of the Women's Cricket Association, June 1930, no. 2. Peterborough: E.M.Barron & Co.

Women's Cricket Association (1954). New Zealand Tour 1954. *Women's Cricket* 19(1).

Women's Cricket Association (1963) *Women's Cricket*. The Official Magazine of the Women's Cricket Association. Mercury Studies: Crawley.

Women's Cricket Association (1970). Yearbook 1970. Women's Cricket Association: Leeds Headingley.

Women's Cricket Associates (2012–2013). International Women's Cricket Council: Third Meeting. Retrieved 7 August 2013, from http://www.womenscrickethistory.org/History/iwcc_3.html

Women's Cricket History (2012–2014). International Women's Cricket Council (IWCC) Fourth Meeting. Retrieved 17 July 2014, from http://www.womenscrickethistory.org/History/iwcc_4.html

Women's Cricket History (2012–2015) 'International Women's Cricket Council (IWCC). http://www.womenscrickethistory.org/History/iwcc.html

Index

Printed and bound in Great Britain by
CPI Group (UK) Ltd, Croydon, CR0 4YY